BLOOD, SWEAT AND HOCKEY

What People Have Said About
Börje Salming

"I felt sorry for him for everything the other teams did to him during the seventies. If they had done that stuff today to any player at all, they would be banned for life."

— *Dave "Tiger" Williams, renowned Leaf fighter*

"Börje was one of the world's greatest hockey players, but he was the world's worst driver. To travel with him was like sailing a boat in stormy water; you either had your nose against the windshield or sat glued to the back of your seat. There were often dents on his cars."

— *Inge Hammarström, Börje's teammate.*

"Circumstances were not right for him. He was a winner, but always surrounded by those who were not."

— *Harry Sinden, former Boston Bruins General Manager*

"We called him King because he was king of all the Europeans. All the players who came over later can thank him for everything."

— *"Tiger" Williams, player, Toronto Maple Leafs*

"The Maple Leafs were a madhouse, so the fans didn't protest when Börje left. If there is anyone on another club who should win the Stanley Cup, it is Börje Salming."

— *Joe Brentwood, taxi driver, Toronto*

"No one mastered the art of sleeping as well as Börje. He gave everything during the games and then was completely wiped. He could sleep anywhere, anytime, anyhow. I know because I woke him up countless times."

— *Inge Hammarström, orderly teammate*

"He can have one of my eyes!"

— *One of the thousands of fans who phoned the hospital when Börje was in danger of losing his sight*

"Few Swedes have really understood what immeasurable popularity he enjoyed during his years in Toronto."

— *Singel Ericson, journalist,* Expressen

"I visited Börje once during the '70s. We went out to buy yogurt for the kids but could find nowhere to park. So Börje double-parked and we rushed into the store. It took a while before we found the yogurt and suddenly we heard a harsh voice: 'Who belongs to the Volvo outside?' A large policeman looked in the shop.
'It's mine,' answered Börje, and started for the door to go and move the car.
'Oh, Mr. Salming. Take it easy. No problem. Do your shopping!' When we came out, I understood once and for all that Börje was a superstar in Toronto. The policeman stood and directed the traffic around Börje's Volvo."

— *Sven-Åke Svensson, a friend from Kiruna*

"Only a handful of players have reached Börje Salming's level: Gordie Howe, Bobby Orr, Phil Esposito, Guy Lafleur, Marcel Dionne and Wayne Gretzky. Salming's genial play could transform the most boring match into a memory for life."

— *Jim Proudfoot, reporter,* Toronto Star

"Salming cornered me and asked me why I wrote negatively. He listened and then said calmly: 'I only wanted to know, we all have a reason for the things we do. Sometimes we just have a bad day, we are under pressure...'"

— *Bill Houston, journalist,* Globe and Mail

"Sometimes it was hard to go out with the guys after games. I drank a light beer that lasted the whole evening, then I had to pay. It was pretty expensive."

— *Inge Hammarström, an abstemious teammate*

"He was often sick and I ran after him with medicine, so I was surprised that he played for so long. Although not really, he was unbelievably stubborn and keen to train."

— *Rune Lantto, coach Kiruna AIF*

"A few months before training camp, Börje rang and asked for photos and names of all the players. He didn't want to come home as a diva and not know the guys' names."

— *A secret source, AIK's office*

"I wouldn't swap Börje Salming for the godfather himself."

— *Harold Ballard, Maple Leafs' owner*

"A team is exactly like anywhere else where many people work together. There's talk about other people. But I have never heard Börje say a bad word about any other person, although he's not frightened to say exactly what he thinks.
Already at 20, he possessed a kind of built-in authority and natural disrespect for most things. Thure Wickberg [the chairman of Brynäs] controlled Brynäs with an iron grip and was not a person whom many dared question.
Before an away match, Thure stated:
"Time is so limited that we won't have time to eat after the match. Instead, we have decided to eat sandwiches on the bus."
No one said anything, except Börje, who slowly lifted his head and asked:
"Who are 'we'?!""

— *Tommy Sandlin, trainer for Brynäs and Tre Kronor*

BÖRJE
SALMING

BLOOD, SWEAT AND HOCKEY

Börje Salming with Gerhard Karlson

HarperCollins*Publishers*Ltd

To Margitta, Anders and Teresa.
Without you there would be no book.

Photo credits: cover photo/Mr. Magnus Mårding; back cover
photo/Mr. Graig Abel; photo insert 1, 2, 3/private; 4/H. Lundborg; 5, 6,
7, 8, 9, 10/private; 11, 12, 13, 14, 15, 16/Mr. Graig Abel.

Extracts from William Houston's book *Ballard: A Portrait of Canada's
Most Controversial Sports Figure*, published in 1985, used with permission of the author.

First English Edition

Canadian Cataloguing in Publication Data

Salming, Börje
    Blood, sweat and hockey

Translation of Blod, svett och hockey.
Includes index.
ISBN 0-00-215840-X

1. Salming, Börje. 2. National Hockey League — Biography. 3. Hockey
players — Canada — Biography. 4. Swedes — canada — Biography. I.
Karlsson, Gerhard. II. Title.

GV848.5.S3A313 1991   796.962'092   C91-094901-8

91 92 93 94 95 AG 5 4 3 2 1

Contents

Introduction

by Alan Eagleson

Billy Harris, the coach of the Swedish National Team, introduced me to Börje Salming at the 1972 World Championships in Prague.

Billy was a former NHL player and a good friend of mine. He told me that Börje would be a great player in the NHL. I saw Börje play in that tournament and he was everything Billy Harris said he was. Börje could skate like the wind, make passes like Bobby Orr, and change the pace of the game to suit himself.

Börje came to the NHL in 1973 and became an All-Star defenceman for the Toronto Maple Leafs. I live in Toronto and I had the chance to see Börje in action on many occasions. He and Inge Hammarström were the first Swedes to prove to the NHL that Swedish players could play on an equal basis with the best players in the world.

Börje and his wife and family made Toronto their home for nearly twenty years. We will miss them all, not only because we will miss Börje's hockey skills, but also because we are losing his contribution to our community. Börje was always happy to help any charitable cause. His teammates enjoyed every aspect of his personality and Toronto hockey fans loved him.

Börje was a leader for Swedish players in the NHL and in international hockey. In the 1976 Canada Cup, he led Sweden to a third-place finish and was named an All-Star Canada Cup defenceman, along with Bobby Orr.

Everyone involved in hockey in North America wishes Börje success in his return to Sweden. Börje set a very high standard for every Swedish player who hopes to play in the NHL.

Good luck, Börje.

R. Alan Eagleson
Executive Director
National Hockey League Players' Association

Foreword

I t wasn't until the early spring of 1990 that I knew for sure that this book would be written, although the idea had existed for some time. The big question was would Börje Salming want to write a book, and, most of all, would he be willing to reveal the reality behind the headlines rather than the disjointed impressions that newspaper articles usually give us.

I wrote a letter and then phoned Börje in Detroit. At first, he was reserved and sounded rather doubtful. He did not seem particularly keen to star in a book, but he promised to let me know his decision anyway.

Several months passed before the telephone rang late one evening. It was Börje. In his slightly cracked voice, he asked if it was really true that I wanted to come over to Canada to gather material for a book about him.

I said yes, and it was settled. All that was left after the telephone conversation were many months of work, both with Börje and his family and with the many people who have known him or met him over the years.

For most of us interested in sports, Börje Salming is something of a living legend—a guy who came from nowhere (sorry Kiruna!), broke into the elite ranks with the Brynäs championship team, and a few years later was named the world's best defenceman at the 1973 World Cup in Moscow. He then signed a gold-plated professional contract and disappeared from sight for those of us at home in Sweden.

We heard that his career went well in the NHL, but not until the 1976 Canada Cup did we grasp how well-known and well-loved he had become in Canada, hockey's homeland. When Tre Kronor, the Swedish national team, lined up against the USA in Maple Leaf Gardens, Börje's home arena, we gazed in wonder at our TV screens as the applause for him seemed never-ending.

Since then, we have learned more about the NHL, thanks to all the Swedes who have followed in Börje's footsteps, and we know that the saying, "blood, sweat, and tears," is not just a myth.

Börje represented the Toronto Maple Leafs for 16 years, an unusually long time in a show business-like sporting world where players are well-paid but largely treated as products that can be bought and sold.

In his seventeenth and final year in the NHL (the 1989/1990 season), at the age of 38, Salming played for the Detroit Red Wings. A last insurance year, everyone thought.

Instead Börje moved home to Sweden and signed with AIK. Many of us shook our heads in disbelief, but I have since learned that Börje Salming is not like other athletes. Even though his greatest years are behind him, it was no worn-out wreck who came home, but a man with an incredible physique and an agile body. Motivation is all he needs to play for several more years.

His body was the first thing that struck me when I travelled to Toronto in the spring of 1990 to meet Börje. He still has the body of a well-trained 25-year-old. Newspaper photos that show only a scarred face and knocked-out teeth are not particularly fair. I was met by an agile and suntanned guy who hopped in and out of his car without any visible ailments.

I cannot pretend that I know Börje inside out, but, after nearly a year working together, my picture of him is clear: Börje is an ordinary guy from Norrland, but an unusually skillful hockey defenceman who experienced a tremendous amount during his 17 years in the NHL—both positive and negative. He may sometimes seem to be laidback and relaxed, but he is loyal and steadfast when he has promised something. He does not boast about his successes, but he is in some way boyishly proud of his achievements over the years. It is no surprise that he keeps Wayne Gretzky's signed hockey stick at home in the cellar!

We have worked hard pulling the story of his life together from memories, newspaper clippings, and history books. Sometimes the work felt never-ending to me. Börje is not a person who tells things first off in an engaging and detailed way.

But all he needed was time. He had simply never thought that his splendid hockey career was much to talk about. Sports might seem a bit petty in the light of today's unhappy world, but they are still a more humane and healthier form of entertainment than most of what streams out of our television sets.

After the work on this book and all the attention from the media that he has had since he returned to Sweden, Börje realizes that he has become a Swedish legend whether he wants to be or not. I can detect a fair amount of joy behind his shyness. We have not forgotten this great fighter!

Many people have gladly discussed and contributed old memories to help Börje and me with this book. Therefore, in conclusion, I'd like to extend a grateful thank you to the following people: Karin, Margitta, Isak, and Stig Salming, Inge Hammarström, Ulf Jansson, Rune Lantto, Dan Dyer, Bill Houston, Björn Wagnsson, Ken Olofsson, Hasse Andersson, Sven-Åke Svensson, and John-Ivar Larsson.

Gerhard Karlsson, January 1991

P.S.   The italicized introductions in certain chapters
        are notes from me as co-author.

For those of you who are not familiar with Swedish hockey, the NHL, or hockey terms, a short glossary is found at the end of the book.

1

The Salming Brothers

They called the Salming brothers crazy. They said we fought and scared the hell out of everyone on the ice.

During the early seventies, opposing teams and spectators had little affection for Stig and me. And, to be honest, we were no angels. We detested "big mouths" and bullies, something left over from our tough childhood in Kiruna. We always stood up for each other, especially Stig for me. Because we played for Brynäs, Sweden's top club, which had half the national team in its lineup, we expected opposing teams to try to throw us off our game by hooking, holding, and whacking us at every opportunity.

Sometimes it worked. On one occasion, we needed a police escort to escape the Timra arena. Timrå's team was tough, big, and mean, with hysterical fans who hated the Salming brothers. Each time I touched the puck, the crowd let out loud, persistent boos.

Midway through the final period of one game, the Timrå players tired of merely shouting abuse and began taking aim at us with sticks and elbows. Finally, a fight erupted. The referee quickly lost control of the game and was knocked down by a Timrå player. As I skated off the ice, past the Timrå bench, the giant forward Finn Lundström leaned over the boards and screamed: "Don't get so bloody uptight, Salming!"

I turned and knocked him out with a straight right.

The referee, unimpressed with my punching prowess, tossed me out of the game.

The dressing room was in a shed outside the arena. As I began to stroll towards the door, I quickly realized I was being followed. There were almost eight thousand spectators in the arena and the angriest among them seemed determined to exact their own justice. Decking big Lundström was one thing; facing a mob was another. I started to run for the shed. All that separated the mob from the changing rooms was a rope barrier. I had no protection. I rushed into the room and banged the door behind me.

"Come out and we'll make mincemeat of you!" they shouted.

They screamed other threats and insults, too, but after a while I dared to peek out and saw a guard struggling to hold them back. Seconds later I heard a crash as the window in the door smashed into a thousand pieces. Soon the police arrived. They waited until the game ended, then formed a human barrier stretching from the shed to our bus. We escaped in one piece, but the mob made it clear we would not be welcome in Sundsvall again.

Looking into the hate-filled eyes of that angry mob was the most frightening experience of my career. The only episode that came close was a shootout at the old Detroit

Olympia arena following a game in the late seventies, but it was unrelated to hockey.

The Olympia, since demolished, was in the heart of one of Detroit's toughest downtown neighborhoods, a slum where muggings and robberies are common. As usual, I was the last player changed after the game. As I came rushing out of the old arena to catch the waiting team bus, a man suddenly grabbed me and yanked me back inside.

"Get down," he shouted.

Seconds later gunshots rang out.

Police were shooting at a screeching getaway car. My teammates, trapped on the bus, were terrified, but fortunately no one was injured. This was the closest I came to the violence that infects most large American cities. Today the Red Wings play in a modern complex called the Joe Louis Arena. It is located on the river front, a part of town that is safer—and quieter.

After the disorderly match in Timrå, Stig took me aside on the bus for some stern words. He snarled that I had behaved badly. It made no sense, he said, to lose my cool in a game that we'd won easily, 7-1, especially with the playoffs fast approaching.

"You understand you'll be suspended now!" he scolded.

And Stig, as usual, was right.

*   *   *

In my youth, I was never one to ponder the ways of the world. I've never been much of a philosopher. But the passing years, and to some extent fatherhood, have helped me see the forces that shaped my life. My self-confidence and will to win come from Stig. He taught me not with words but by example. His companionship has meant an

9

enormous amount to me. He has been my big brother, my friend, and, often, the father I lost as a child.

I was five when my father died in the mine. At the time, the family was told only that there had been an accident. It wasn't until many years later that we learned his skull was crushed when he became stuck on a conveyor belt.

Stig was only nine, yet he willingly accepted responsibility for his kid brother. Naturally, I looked up to him and wanted to do everything he did. Oh, how I worshipped him. He was daring and successful at whatever enterprise he tried. I wanted to be like him, but often I ended up running in tears to my mother. At least, that's how it went for the first ten years.

Stig was hard on me, but God help anyone else who treated me unkindly. Never hesitant to defend his little brother, Stig could appear nasty if he wanted to. His dark hair, sharp contours, and thick eyebrows gave him a natural look of authority.

Swedish newspapers have called him "Stygge Stigge" (Nasty Stig), but that's unfair. Stig is a loving family man with a good heart. That may sound amusing to those frightened on the ice by Stig, but it's true. Reputations, however, are tough to change.

Even as children we were known as the notorious wild Salmings from Kiruna. But we were about the same as everyone else. Perhaps the difference was that we were always together and easily recognized. Our mother had knitted us identical red sweaters that we often wore. They kept us warm, but made us stand out whenever mischief was on our minds.

I remember little about my father, Erland, but my mother says that every day Stig and I waited by the door until he came home from the mine. Father would have his lunchbox in his hand, ready to share some saved tidbit. My mother was always home to take care of us, but in the weeks after my father died it was difficult for her to cope with the demands of two energetic boys while also grieving for her lost husband.

Her mother stepped in. "Now you send Börje to us and then find yourself a job. Don't sit at home and brood," she said.

My grandmother was right. Mother needed a chance to get out of the house and rebuild her life. This was impossible, however, with a five-year-old son tying her down. So I was sent to live with my grandparents. I understood little of what had happened. First my father disappeared, and then I was forced to leave my mother and Stig. It seemed unfair. But life was good in Murjek, just outside Boden, with my grandparents Edla and Fredrik. When Mother found a waitressing job, I moved back home.

Mother comes from Vassijaure, home of Sweden's most northern railway station. Father was the son of Anders Nikolaus, a tradesman who settled in the village of Salmi at the southern edge of Lake Talojärvi, not far from Torne Lake. My father's family struggled hard to build a decent life. My paternal grandparents had twelve children, six of whom died.

Grandfather was a Lapp who had reindeer in the mountains, but he also had a nose for business. Although Salmi only comprised five homesteads, grandfather ran a village shop. He built a couple of small sawmills, fished, and provided a taxi service. He was determined, worked extremely hard, and was regarded as the boss in the neighborhood.

Grandfather was religious, a "Lestadian," a member of a sect that has strong beliefs about right and wrong. I think he disapproved of Stig and me because we occasionally answered him back and were a bit lazy. But young boys neither want to spend their waking hours doing chores nor sitting in a church and crying on Sundays. Religion, I suppose, can give comfort and be a positive experience, but the Lestadians always seemed so unhappy on Sundays.

We had our own ideas of fun. I spent many summers around Salmi and they were filled with adventures in the wilderness. I fished and hunted grouse in the forest with Stig and Uncle Isak. Once we blocked a creek with our fishing net and caught so much salmon in two days that we could hardly carry it all home. It was great fun, although I hope net fishing is forbidden now.

*   *   *

After a few years my mother married my father's brother, Isak. The union, welcomed by Stig and me, seemed natural because Isak had always looked out for us like a father. He was a hard man, but fair. Soon the family had a new member when my little sister, Carina, was born. We lived in a small house on Matojärvi Street in Kiruna, not exactly poor but not well-off either.

Stig and I never worried much about money. All we thought about were sports: soccer, handball, wrestling, field hockey and, our first love, ice hockey. Because I followed my older brother everywhere, I was often the smallest person on the ice. The bigger boys never excluded me. Instead they stuck me in a position that no one else would play—goaltender.

I never complained. On the contrary, it was great to be involved, to be in the midst of the action, throwing myself back and forth to stop the puck. Years later I used the skills honed in those backyard games to help me block shots in the NHL. Funny, but I have never been afraid to throw myself in front of the puck.

After school, we would rush straight for the Matojärvis hockey rink. (We lived next to the sports centre.) We'd take a short break when Mother called us for dinner and then head back out again to play until dark. Throughout my teen years, school and homework were unimportant to me. All that mattered was hockey.

Some days I played handball, but it never equalled the pleasure of hockey. Inevitably, we'd leave the handball court and go back to the rink to play for as long as daylight permitted. We'd play with or without skates; it didn't really matter to us.

*   *   *

"What do you think you're doing out there?"

Rune Lantto's deep voice echoed in the empty arena. It was Christmas and the rink was closed, but I had crept in beneath the stands, put on my skates, and was skating in the dark. Rune thought I was overdoing it, but he was always kind to me. He understood that I was a harmless kid who was crazy about hockey.

"I'm practising," I yelled back.

Rune laughed. He was the coach of Kiruna AIF, but he was much more than that to our family. I was often sick with colds and sinusitis and Rune would bring me medicine. I would lie between the sheets worrying not about falling behind in my school work, but about missing hockey practice. It happened more than once that I invented a sudden recovery just so I could get back on the ice.

My hockey allegiance was to AIF, the workers' sports club. It competed against IFK, the civil servants' and engineers' club. Today the clubs are combined. But back then, a merger was as impossible as driving a car to the moon. Neither club wanted anything to do with the other. It all seemed silly to me. I just wanted to play hockey, have fun, and stay out of all the sideline squabbling. It was impossible to avoid altogether, however, because one of my best friends, Rolf Älvero, played for IFK. At first I was bothered by the teasing I endured because of our friendship, but eventually I learned to ignore it. Why shouldn't we be friends? We played field hockey and soccer together and had fun. It was only during Derby matches that we went our separate ways and I cheered like mad for the yellow, black, and white AIF team. I lost touch with Rolf when I moved to Toronto, but I know he played for the elite series team Björklöven from Umeå during their best years in the eighties. Not bad for an IFK supporter.

Even though I was only a junior and too small to make the team myself, I seldom missed an A-team practice. Stig was on the team and I dreamed of someday joining him.

The A-team practised first, followed by the juniors. But I would nag my brother to help me sneak a few minutes with his team. I'd change like a flash in the juniors' room and then slide nonchalantly onto the ice with the A-team as it circled the ice during its warm-up. I'd melt into the waves of players skating round and round the ice, being careful not to get in anyone's way.

After a few minutes, Rune Lantto or Stig Engström blew the coach's whistle and I bolted from the ice like lightning.

To fill the time until the juniors' practice, I latched on to the rink attendant, Karl-Erik Nyberg, and helped him with his chores. I taped sticks, filled water bottles, fetched towels, and ran all types of errand. My reward was the occasional broken stick, which was perfect for field hockey. I always kept an eye on what was happening on the ice, and occasionally I was allowed to join in if the A-team was short of players. Then I was king.

*   *   *

I don't know if I had the most talent, but my enthusiasm was unmatched. I would have played hockey twenty-four hours a day if it were possible. The practices were nearly as much fun as the games. I always enjoyed pushing myself to the limit. In fact, I still do.

I enjoy working out and keeping my body fit. To spice exercise with intense competition, to sweat beside your teammates and give everything to try to win, is the best feeling I know. I guess it sounds strange that a 40-year-old who has played hockey from childhood still thinks the game is fun. People assume I continue to play for the money, and it's true that I've been well-paid. But there's more to it than that.

Sure, money has been important to me during the past ten years. After every season, I seriously considered retiring. I asked myself if all the effort, travelling, and time away from my family was really worth it. Then I'd be offered $350,000 a year to continue. Money like that is difficult to turn down.

Still, there's more to it than cash.

I still enjoy playing. I still love the rush of adrenalin that competition brings, the excitement and the challenge. I still treasure the camaraderie of the dressing room. I have spent thousands of hours on the ice. My coaches have always played me a lot, which suits me. I wouldn't continue if my role was to sit on the bench like a relic from the past. I want to play.

Sometimes I wonder, of course, if it isn't time I grew up, because in many respects I've lived in an unreal world. But every time I think seriously of quitting, someone offers me a new contract. I have never had to go looking for a spot on a team, and big money has always been involved. So I ask myself: Why should I quit?

What would I do instead?

I still enjoy playing hockey. I'm well-paid, in good physical shape, able to meet lots of interesting people, and have a long vacation to spend with my family. How many jobs offer all that?

Naturally, there are also disadvantages, but the advantages have always outweighed them. Hockey may be the only job I can do really well. I've been in no hurry to walk away from it to start anew. Perhaps I am also a little scared about what I'll do after hockey. Financial security is important, but maintaining a sense of fulfillment is equally important. I suspect that the majority of successful people feel the same way. Once a person has attained economic freedom, the small everyday events become more important. Without money worries, a person can continue to do a job simply because it is fun and personally fulfilling. That's what hockey has become for me. So I'm nervous about giving it up.

I can picture myself staying in hockey in some capacity, but definitely not as an elite coach. I'd prefer to work with youngsters, building something from the beginning and watching it grow and develop through hours of practice until finally all the energy is channelled into producing a positive result.

I have witnessed too much behind-the-scenes manoeuvering to aspire to the position of elite coach. A coach has too little time to devote to hockey because he has to waste too much energy defending himself to the press, club directors, and fans. Becoming involved in that type of nonsense is the closest thing I know to hell. I'd quickly become fed up and angry. I lack the patience and thick skin that a coach needs to cope with the everyday pressures of his thankless job. A player can relieve pressure by practising hard and playing physical matches, but a coach must pay the price in sleepless nights.

Good coaches have my greatest respect. I can't understand how they handle the frustration that must come from continually defending and explaining their actions.

The job of coach sometimes attracts guys who like the sound of their own voices and have little skill or knowledge of the game. Confronted with questions and criticism, their response is to stand and shout. Unfortunately, I have encountered a few of that type, mostly in Canada where hockey may be big, but where the education of coaches is not particularly well-developed. It has improved in Canada, but Swedish coaches are certainly better at getting their message across to the players. There ought to be a demand for Swedish coaches in the NHL, but, unfortunately, any coach who tests those waters should expect a stormy ride without trustworthy friends.

I played under nine NHL coaches. A couple I hardly remember, while some I remember for reasons other than hockey. For example, there was Mike Nykoluk and his never-ending cigars. He was a nice guy, a pleasant man in an unpleasant profession. Some coaches screamed from their first day until the day they were fired. John Brophy was like that, an expert at scaring the young players half to death. Dan Maloney was another loudmouth. Mostly, though, the coaches were ordinary guys trying to perform a difficult job as best they could.

Tommy Sandlin, my coach in Brynäs, is the best coach I played for, with Roger Neilson a close second. Both have been criticized for being too theoretical, but a player needs a serious coach who does more than just scream and shout when things go poorly. When a team is struggling, a coach must be able to relax, step back, and analyze the situation to find something new and positive.

Tommy is able to make practices varied and fun, which is important because elite hockey means practice, practice, and practice some more. Repeating the same tired drills over and over is boring and dulls enthusiasm. Tommy also has a knack for promoting team spirit. He lets us play our game without worrying about the coach trying to show off. For example, instead of simply telling the team how to play, Tommy gathers each five-man unit together to discuss tactics. Each player is invited to participate in the development of the strategy, while Tommy interjects his tips and comments. Clever. Every player feels he is involved in the game plan. If the strategy fails, no one can sit back and grumble, "Damn, it was the coach's fault."

In Canada, this simple but ingenious coaching method is uncommon. In Sweden, it is popular with most teams.

Stig tried coaching, and I believe his players liked him, but the other pressures of the job gave him grey hairs. He is like me. Neither of us enjoys the limelight. In fact, I hate it.

Even after all my years in the game, I can worry for several days over an upcoming television appearance or some other official function. I have improved over the years, but I have always avoided the spotlight as much as possible, which has probably cost me a lot of money. I had an advertising agent in Canada for a while and he nagged me to accept interviews and to try to appear on television as much as possible. He must have been disappointed in me.

Above all, I was handicapped by my imperfect command of English, so I did anything to avoid television appearances and only gave a few interviews. It was a luxury I could afford because I made good money by simply playing the game. I didn't need the extra exposure and outside income, so I saw no need to get involved in something I didn't enjoy. The advertising agent gave up after a few years.

2
Farewell to the Mine

"Börje, now is your chance. We're playing an exhibition game against the national team and the Brynäs management wants to take a look at you." Stig's voice on the telephone didn't sound particularly excited. It didn't need to be. I was the one walking on cloud nine.

I was eighteen and my dream was about to come true. If Brynäs from Gävle, Sweden's best hockey team, was interested in me, I was ready for the big time.

In AIF, two defencemen ranked high among Sweden's juniors, Per-Olof Usitalo and Börje Salming. Usitalo was considered a little better than me, and I later learned that Brynäs's scout in Norrbotten, Henning Nilsson, thought Brynäs would choose him. Stig probably put in a good word for me. It was the spring of 1969 when I boarded the train for the 1,000 kilometre trek south. I was nervous but, having played for the junior national team, I felt well-prepared. I told myself that this was just one step up, not a mountain to climb. I also drew comfort from knowing that Stig had been with Brynäs for the past two years.

I was fortunate to have him there.

I quietly eyed the well-known players in the changing room as I pulled on my borrowed Brynäs sweater. But in my haste I overlooked one important detail. On the way out, Stig passed me and nodded at the tail I was dragging behind me.

"You'd better learn to put on your suspenders, too," he said, smiling.

Out on the ice, things went better. I played with Brynäs captain and defenceman, Lasse Bylund and held my own. I still remember clearly what happened afterwards. It was not particularly sensational, nor were any great words spoken. There was no talk of a contract or money—it didn't work that way then. No, what has stuck in my mind is a short sentence from coach Thure Wickberg.

"Well, Börje," he said, "tomorrow you can come and collect a team jacket."

With the team jacket and a new pair of playboy shoes, I returned to Kiruna. I was satisfied and my appetite had been whetted. I had played beside and against national-team players and found them to be good, but not supermen. I felt I belonged with them.

Many of them—Lars-Göran Nilsson, Tord Lundstöm, and my brother—came from Kiruna.

After that one game, the mine seemed a long way away. I knew then that I would be able to make my mother happy by fulfilling the only demand she ever made of her sons: "You must never work in the mine!"

Her request might sound simple, but in Kiruna at that time, young men had nowhere to work but in the mine. It has been suggested that aversion to the mine provided extra motivation for the dozens of talented athletes who grew up in Kiruna. In Swedish elite hockey alone, between 30 and 40 top players have come from my home town.

Supposedly, these athletes were alike in that every one of them saw hockey as a one-way ticket out of town. "Practise hard so you can leave here," was the presumed rallying cry.

But I've never believed that young athletes think that way. I know I didn't.

My theory is that Kiruna produced a disproportionate number of athletes because there was nothing else to do in town besides sport. It was hard, cold, and dark, and if you wanted to have fun you had to make it yourself. And sport is fun. If you play at it long enough, eventually you get good. Ice hockey is the type of sport where you can reach a high level simply by developing your talents, particularly skating. Complement natural ability with organized training and determination and a good athlete can become an elite one. But it takes hours upon hours of repetition, a lot of patience and a lot of time. There was no shortage of time in Kiruna.

*   *   *

I still lived at home in 1967. I had left school and started workshop training, but my interests were elsewhere. Hockey was my passion, one that became even more inflamed when I was nominated for Norrbotten's TV-Puck-Team*. It was there that I first met Anders Hedberg. Hedberg, a national team hero who went on to star with the Winnipeg

---

* Swedish television broadcasts a national competition for district junior teams, called TV-Puck-Team.

Jets of the WHA and the New York Rangers of the NHL, is now the club director of AIK and my present employer. Even then he was regarded as a wonder boy. He played for MoDo and represented Ångermanland in the TV-Puck. And of course he was good.

Anders scored five goals against us in the TV-Puck match which Ångermanland won 6-0. We all thought the coaches were overdoing it a bit when he was flown by chartered plane immediately after the game to his elite series debut the same day. And maybe we were a little jealous as well. A few hours after our match he scored his first goal against AIK's goalie Leif "Honken" Holmqvist.

Talk about a wonder boy. Talk about success.

Eventually, Hedberg became one of the best-paid players in the NHL. In 1978, he joined with Ulf "Lill-Pröjsarn" Nilsson to sign a two-year deal with the Rangers worth $850,000. At the time, it was a spectacular contract for a free agent, but totally in keeping with Anders's good fortune. Anders is a player who has matched all the lofty expectations he has carried since childhood.

Meanwhile, while Hedberg was scoring five goals, not many eyebrows were lifted for Börje Salming. But I did well enough to be chosen to go to a training camp for the best defencemen in the TV-Puck. Then things began to happen. I got the chance to play on AIF's A-team in Division 2 and teamed with Stig for eight games before he signed with Brynäs and moved to Gävle.

*   *   *

The next spring I encountered Hedberg again, this time as a teammate. We represented Sweden in the junior European Cup in Garmisch Partenkirchen, West Germany, and the tournament went well for both of us—and for the whole team. We placed second.

I was keen about hockey long before the West German trip, but afterwards I was totally enthralled by the game and the opportunities it presented. To play alongside so many good players and receive first-class instruction from top coaches was a great experience. And we had fun. It was wonderful to ride a horse-drawn sleigh in the beautiful Alps.

The following year, 1969, I was a regular with the AIF team, as well as holding my spot on the junior national team. There were a lot of games and travel.

AIF's nearest opponent was in Boden, 330 kilometres away. During the long journeys, I learned to sleep in any position. I was also working in the mine's service workshop. It wasn't uncommon for a work day to follow a tough away game. After the short trip to Boden we got home about 2:30 a.m., but we wouldn't arrive back from any of the other cities before daylight. The company was generous with time off, but nevertheless I occasionally showed up for work tired. On those days I would sneak away for catnaps behind a handy crate in the workshop. Once, the foreman found me while I slept and was unimpressed by my explanation.

He mocked me. "You'll be sorry," he said. "You're never going to make a living playing hockey."

My stay in the workshop was short. I worked for a month, then the company went on strike for two months. I went back for one more month before Brynäs called and I moved to Gävle in the spring of 1970.

I played my last match for Kiruna on March 14, 1970. According to the newspaper clippings, we lost 7-5 in the first district final against Boden's BK. Then I was off to the big city.

Wickberg, Brynäs's manager, personally phoned my mother to reassure her that her boy would be well-treated and that she needn't be concerned. But my mother turned out to be the least of Wickberg's worries. He had a tougher time, through his negotiator Breit Hellman, settling on a transfer fee with Rune Lantto in Kiruna.

Because Brynäs was a prestigious team and accustomed to getting its way, Hellman's first offer to Kiruna's management was low.

"We'll give you ten thousand [crowns, about $1,400] for Börje, our normal transfer fee for young players," Hellman told Lantto over the phone.

"Never," replied Lantto. "We're willing to release Börje, but not for such a piddling amount."

After a couple weeks of fruitless negotiations, Wickberg called Rune.

"I hear that you and Breit can't reach an agreement," Wickberg said.

"That's right," said Rune. "You have to understand our position. We can't afford to lose good, young players without fair compensation. We know Kiruna is regarded as a training ground, but to continue we must have money to survive. It's to your advantage, too. It costs a lot to be located so far away from other teams."

"So what'll it take to get Salming?" said Wickberg.

"Twenty-five to thirty thousand."

"Okay, then, it's a deal."

Two weeks later the transfer papers were signed beside a road in the middle of nowhere. Brynäs sent Henry Jansson, a board member and avid fisherman, to sign for the team. He was a friend of Henning Nilsson, the Brynäs scout who lived in Vuollerim. There are 350 kilometres between Vuollerim and Kiruna. Jansson, anxious to go fishing, made it as far as Nilsson's home in Vuollerim and then he phoned Lantto in Kiruna. "Rune, it's such a long drive all the way up to Kiruna. We want to go fishing in Stora Lulevattnet, so how about meeting us along the way? We'll pay for your gas."

Rune agreed and drove 250 kilometres to meet Jansson at the Porjus crossroads. There my transfer papers were signed and I officially became a member of Brynäs IF.

Rune was probably satisfied. No manager likes to lose his top young players, but Rune was a realist and understood that he could never build an elite team in Kiruna. The map told him how unrealistic it was to put a team in the far north, particularly in a town with no outside jobs other than those in the mine.

Two years later Lantto and Wickberg met at a hockey conference in Stockholm.

"I wanted you to hear it from me," Thure said. "We have sold Börje to Toronto."

3

Attention,
Brynäs!

On April 12, 1970, I signed with Brynäs. At first I lived in
Sätra with Stig and his wife Lena, but I soon moved into a
tiny flat on Köpmannagatan 13D, where several Brynäs
players had lived before me.

I had had nothing to do with the deal between AIF and
Brynäs. Brynäs found me the flat, kept me busy, and paid
me 1,000 crowns a month, about $145.

Back then I wasn't particularly responsible—I took
every day as it came. Team management and Stig looked
after me and made sure that I didn't waste my days. The
problem was filling the hours between practices. School
was one option, but I wasn't interested in the classroom.
Thure Wickberg was the head of his own plumbing company and gave me work that first summer as a handyman,
working on the house of his son, Håkan, a member of the
national team.

Thure was a great guy, authoritative but with a big heart. I learned a lot working for him. He was a responsible 60-year-old businessman and I was a greenhorn kid whose greatest interest was in having fun. But we hit it off together and it was a very valuable summer for me.

Thure had contacts in high places. When I was called up for military service, he pulled a few strings to keep me near his hockey club. I had been assigned to I19 in Boden, but somehow ended up at I14 in Gävle. It was Thure's doing, but don't ask me how.

I was happy in Brynäs. In retrospect, it provided an excellent training ground for my eventual career in the NHL, although I never suspected as much at the time. I had no ambition to play professionally in North America. It was practically unheard of for any European to go abroad to play hockey, and even less likely for a lean defenceman from a remote northern village in Sweden.

No, I aspired to nothing more than a simple career in Sweden's semi-pro elite league, working for Thure during the day, attending practices and games in the evenings, and partying. I wanted few worries and lots of fun. I had no great plans, which bothered Stig. He usually criticized me when I visited him.

"Börje, you will end up as a road sweeper if you don't look out," he'd say. Even hockey-crazed Tommy Sandlin believed I should be building a life outside of hockey.

"What will become of you?" he'd ask.

But I wasn't worried. I believed everything would work out somehow. If I had been injured and my career suddenly ended, I'd probably have taken a job as a welder somewhere in Gävle, which would have been okay too.

The atmosphere in the Brynäs dressing room was special, crude some have said, but we treated each other fairly.

We screamed and shouted a lot, but no one lost sight of our priorities. Hockey and the good of the team always came first. We were determined to be the best team, which meant no one player could become more important than anyone else.

We were a competitive bunch, even amongst ourselves. After practice, if we were on the soccer field outside the rink, we'd race to the dressing room. Each of us had to be first or nothing.

Lennart "Tiger" Johansson, a team veteran, was always playing practical jokes.

In my rookie year, he tricked me into cycling 100 kilometres. Our young goalkeeper, Wille Löfqvist, was another one of Tiger's victims. Wille made his A-team debut in an easy European Cup game against a mediocre Swiss or German team. As the final seconds ticked down, we were leading 14-0 and Wille was getting ready to celebrate a shutout.

Then Tiger got the puck deep in our zone and banged a shot past a startled Wille. We were all dumbfounded.

"We wouldn't want Wille to think he's something special," cracked Tiger as he returned to the bench.

Our practices in Gävle were famous, often attracting as many as 1,500 spectators. At the end of the workout, Sandlin would divide the team in two for a high-paced scrimmage. The action was freewheeling and often as thrilling as a league game. Oh, the battles. Some days it was harder and more prestigious to win the scrimmages than a league game. We'd bet a case of beer and play all out. It was a great feeling to win, crack open a cold beer, and tease the losers.

Sandlin was crafty. He knew how to get the best from each player. To get the most from the Salming brothers he'd put us on opposing teams and let sibling rivalry take

31

over. Stig would tease me relentlessly. When I checked him into the boards, he'd just laugh. "My little brother is really something," he'd joke with the newspaper reporters who were eager to find out about the new Salming.

Kidding aside, though, my play improved quickly when I was reunited with Stig after our two-year separation. He had always brought out the best in me. It was also exciting meeting all the national-team stars and participating in high-level practices. This combination of factors had an explosive impact on my game. I became like the infamous ketchup bottle: after a long wait, success poured out all at once. I made the Brynäs A-team and we won the Swedish Gold Cup. Then, in rapid succession, I was selected to the Vikings, Sweden's national B-team, and then to Tre Kronor, the national team.

The national B-team was led by a Canadian, Des Moroney. It was on his recommendation that I was quickly promoted to Tre Kronor, the pinnacle of achievement for a Swedish hockey player.

"Börje Salming is more Canadian than some Canadians," Moroney said, referring to my physical style of play.

To make my selection to Tre Kronor even more satisfying, I was accompanied by Stig. We both had strong seasons with Brynäs. For me, however, the season was particularly memorable. For the first time in my life I was Stig's equal on the ice. I could stop idolizing him. Instead, we pushed each other to new heights in a friendly rivalry. Stig had always inspired me, but now I was returning the favor. It was good for both of us.

We had started out together as small boys on the neighborhood rink in Kiruna. But the day we truly knew we had made it as hockey players was September 11, 1971, when we pulled on the Tre Kronor sweater of Sweden and made our national-team debut in Stockholm against Czechoslovakia. Stig wore No. 8; I was No. 9.

The "crazy Salming brothers" from Kiruna had become two of Sweden's best hockey players. It felt great.

Despite my quick success, I felt I had more to give. Military service spoiled my concentration during my first season with Brynäs. I was an officer, which seemed like a joke because I have never enjoyed commanding or being commanded. I was 19 years old and had zero interest in the military.

I was not officer material and mostly tried to remain inconspicuous. I enjoyed the tough training regimen only because it helped my hockey. Otherwise, I disliked holding a position of command in the army.

Once the army made me miss a game completely. We were supposed to ski ten kilometres on the five kilometre track through the forest. Along with a friend, I took coffee and magazines and made a camp near the end of the first lap. Our plan was to rest until the group came around again. Then we'd join them for the sprint to the finish.

But we were discovered.

The officer who found us played for Strömsbro, a small team in Gävle. I wonder sometimes if he relished the opportunity to punish a player from famous Brynäs. In any event, he rescinded my leave to play hockey and confined me to a tent for the evening, forcing me to miss our game against Södertälje. I had a radio to keep me company and a guard outside to make sure I stayed put.

It was the perfect punishment for a hockey-crazy kid.

The army was a constant headache. I didn't hit it off with the Seventh Company's commanding officer, Captain Jerrulf, but luckily Wickberg pulled a few more strings. It turned out that the regiment's commanding officer was a

Brynäs fan and a friend of Thure's. He seemed to know everyone in Gävle. In any event, the commander listened to what I had to say, even though Captain Jerrulf certainly had reason to dislike me. The result was a compromise that allowed the captain and me to go separate ways. I joined the Eighth Company.

A short time later, my hockey career nearly ended when I fell off a high fence and landed on my head. To this day I have two bent vertebrae in my neck. But I don't complain. The doctor said I was luck my neck wasn't broken.

The army life wasn't for me. I was better suited to serve my country wearing Sweden's yellow and blue, with skates on my feet and a hockey stick in my hand.

During my first tour with Tre Kronor, rumors began to surface about interested professional buyers from the NHL. But there was all kinds of speculative hockey talk during the early seventies. For instance, stories about the birth of a professional European league were making the rounds. No one, neither players nor management, seemed to know whether or not the talk was true.

Our knowledge of the NHL was equally limited. We'd heard of the violence and brawling, but no one believed that the professional teams were paying much attention to hockey in Sweden. Likewise, playing in North America wasn't an ambition among Swedish players. We all knew what had happened to Ulf Sterner when he crossed the Atlantic.

Sterner was considered a tough player in Sweden, but after five games with the New York Rangers he was demoted to their farm team. He found the NHL dirty, rough, and dishonest. He was ridiculed and targeted for extra physical abuse simply because he was European.

*   *   *

In the spring of 1972, Brynäs won the Swedish Gold Cup for the third consecutive year. I'd been there for two of them. My career was off to a good start—too good in fact. Sure enough, I suffered my first setback that spring.

I was chosen to represent Sweden at the world championship in Prague, playing on a team that included Ulf Sterner and the other big names of Swedish hockey: Lars-Erik Sjöberg, Lars-Göran Nilsson, "Lill-Prosten" Karlsson, Dan Söderström, Arne Carlsson, the Abrahamsson twins, Håkan Wickberg and Tord Lundström to name but a few.

Tre Kronor had a strong team, but I was unable to play with them to the end of the tournament. I broke my little finger and, despite pleas to team doctor Bo-Johan Norlen, was forbidden to continue with it bandaged. The history books tell me that, surprisingly, the Czechs took the gold. Sweden was third.

*   *   *

That year, 1972, was important for hockey worldwide. Until then, the globe was basically divided in two: the Soviets dominated in Europe, while the NHL professionals ignored everyone else, naively comfortable in their supposed superiority. Then events began to unfold in rapid order:

- Czechoslovakia became the world champions.
- Thommie Bergman left Tre Kronor to accept an NHL contract.
- The World Hockey Association was established and quickly entered bidding wars with the NHL for players.
- Talk continued of a European professional league.
- And, finally, Canada and the Soviet Union engaged in their historic summit series.

The eight-game Canada-Soviet series overshadowed all other developments in hockey for years to come. Canada entered the showdown confident of an easy victory. Before the opening match on September 2 in Montreal, interest among the public and the media was intense. Then the superbly conditioned Soviets shocked the hockey world by winning the first game, 7-3. The Canadian press reacted as if war had broken out. One headline the next day covered the entire front page and screamed: WE LOST!

The Canadians had completely underestimated the skills of Ragulin, Lutjenko, Vasiljev, Jakusjev, Charlamov, Petrov, Maltsev, Michailov, and the rest of the Soviets. Most startling was the work of a young goaltender named Vladislav Tretiak. In that opening game, the Soviets out-classed the Canadians in front of their own fans. The shock turned out to be exactly what the Canadians needed.

Canada won Game 2 in Toronto, 4-1, followed by a 4-4 tie in Winnipeg and a 5-3 Soviet victory in Vancouver. The Soviets led the series 2-1-1 when it moved to Moscow.

Back home, a 5-4 victory in Game 5 put the Soviets in the driver's seat. They needed just one more victory from the three remaining games to win the series. It looked like it was all over for Canada. At least, that's what we thought in Sweden. Instead we saw a dramatic display of Canadian determination. Canada won the final three games (3-2, 4-3, and 6-5) and the series to keep their honor intact.

A greater victory, however, was won by the worldwide hockey community. The days of Canadian smugness were gone. The Soviets proved that other nations could play hockey and play it well. From that day on, NHL general managers were forced to recognize Europe as a hockey arena they couldn't afford to ignore.

4

Yes

The hockey world was changed forever by the Canada-Soviet series and the fallout included a sudden interest among NHL clubs in Swedish players. For years in Sweden we had heard myths about NHL supermen. But the 1972 series demonstrated that North American professionals were mortal, just like the rest of us.

On the way to the Soviet Union, Team Canada had stopped in Sweden for two exhibition games against Tre Kronor. We were awed just reading their names in the papers: Ken Dryden, Tony Esposito, Bobby Orr, Brad Park, Phil Esposito, Paul Henderson, Pete and Frank Mahovlich, Stan Mikita, and Bobby Clarke, to name a few. I had never dreamed of playing against them.

Unfortunately, we were still full of wonder when the puck was dropped. It took Canada less than two minutes to open the scoring on a goal by Henderson. After that, however, we settled down and played them evenly for the rest of the game. The only facet of the game in which we were clearly overmatched was the bodychecking, whacking, and tackling.

The rough play was new to us. According to Swedish rules, violent tactics drew penalties. But the referees looked away and we were unprepared to handle it on our own. We lost 4-1.

Before the second game, our coach, Kjell Svensson, ordered us to abandon our passive ways and play an eye-for-an-eye style.

"Don't retreat one centimetre," he said. "We'll play it their way. Just bang away."

What followed was the dirtiest game ever seen in Sweden. Ulf Sterner, in particular, endured the worst assaults, but we weren't intimidated. In fact, we would have won if one of the biggest hockey stars in the NHL, Phil Esposito, hadn't scored with 47 seconds remaining to tie the game, 4-4. Later in my career I encountered Esposito many times.

A few seasons ago, when the Maple Leafs were in New York playing the Rangers, Esposito, who was a color commentator at the time, insulted me on TV when I made an unscheduled visit to the dressing room. We were trailing by two goals with about ten minutes left in the game. "Salming's a quitter, he was always a quitter," Esposito said. "Look at him bailing out of the game."

What Esposito didn't know was that I had only left to have a broken skate blade repaired. I returned quickly and finished the game. Afterwards, when I heard what Esposito had said, I was glad the trainer had worked quickly to fix the skate so I could carry on.

Esposito has had a chip on his shoulder since the 1977 World Championships in Vienna. I didn't play, but Stig had a few run-ins with him, both on and off the ice. The trouble began when Tre Kronor won a pre-tournament exhibition game, 4-2. After that, the Canadians were determined to brawl their way through the tournament, even fighting in corridors and dressing rooms before and after some of the games.

Sweden opened the tournament by beating the Soviets, 4-2. Hours later, Stig and some teammates were watching a replay of the game on television when a group of Canadians showed up at the restaurant. The Swedes cheered every Tre Kronor goal, which seemed to make the Canadians more and more miserable.

I don't know what my brother said, but some comment infuriated a Canadian.

"Fuck you, Salming!" he yelled, rushing at Stig.

He tried to grab Stig and Stig rose from his chair to fight back. At that point, an American bystander got between them and others rushed in to break them apart. That was the end of the altercation. But throughout the tournament the Canadians behaved so badly and took so many violent penalties that they were severely criticized by the Canadian press.

Paul Henderson was a true gentleman. He was a smooth skater and puckhandler who never shied from physical play and had a natural goal scoring touch. When I moved to Toronto, we became teammates and friends.

Henderson also had a strong will to win. It's no coincidence that he scored the winning goals in each of the last three games against the Soviets. His series-clinching goal, scored with 34 seconds remaining in the final game, made him a legend in Canada. If the Soviets had held on to a 5-5 tie, they would have won the series based on a better goal average. Instead, Henderson made it 6-5 and all of Canada rejoiced in front of their television sets.

It was during these months that I started to wonder—or perhaps dream is a better word—about the NHL.

Of course the Canadians were good, and of course they played a tough, physical style, but they were just hockey players. Up close, the biggest difference between them and us seemed to be that some of them played without helmets.

*   *   *

The autumn of '72 was certainly eventful. The Canadians had stoked the first embers of hope in Swedish players. But, beyond hockey, these were interesting days because of happenings off the ice. I bought Stefan "Lill-Prosten" Karlsson's two-room flat on the south side of Gävle. The flat-warming party proved most interesting. "Lill-Prosten" and "Kulan" (the Ball), otherwise known as my best friend Örjan Persson, were there with their friend Thomas Wendin. The three of them always formed a fun combination, but on this night they led me to a very beautiful young lady—Margitta.

Wendin was Margitta's brother and Margitta was Miss Gävle, which was all the introduction I needed before I started flirting. A few weeks later, we were an item.

My good fortune followed me on the ice. Brynäs was practically unbeatable in the autumn and we were everyone's favorite for the Swedish gold title.

Our team never looked stronger. During the Christmas break we planned to polish our game against a Canadian amateur team on tour in Sweden. Unfortunately, there was more slashing and hacking than polishing. In the midst of one commotion, I threw a tantrum and flattened the referee. It was stupid of me, but it was the third time

I had played against a team whose players wielded their sticks like weapons.

They were also mouthy. It was only an exhibition game during the Christmas break, and it was only a Canadian amateur team, the Barrie Flyers, but maybe it became nasty when they encountered two bull-headed brothers from Kiruna. Stig and I refused to back down and we gave as good as we got. I had learned that much from the autumn matches against Team Canada. Maybe that's why Toronto Maple Leafs' scout Gerry McNamara noticed me.

He was in the stands when we played the Canadians in Gävle. After getting tossed by the referee, I strolled alone to the dressing room and threw my stick in a corner.

"Damn fools," I muttered.

A man dressed in a smart overcoat with a suit and tie followed me through the door. I had never seen him before.

"Would you like to come to Canada to play for the Toronto Maple Leafs?" There I stood, the kid with the worst English in the class, who now needed it most.

"Yes..."

That's all I said. It was the only English I knew. The man shook my hand and left.

I just stood there, alone in the room, questions filling my head. Me a professional?

"Oh, my God!"

I was in a slight state of shock, feeling exhilarated and dumbfounded at the same time. I sat on the wooden bench and leaned against the wall. "What do I do now?"

I sat there for a long time, just thinking. Thoughts swirled around my head like October leaves blowing across a lawn. I'd have to learn English. I could earn lots of money. The NHL is brutal. What about farm teams...?

I later learned how McNamara found me. He was in Sweden to look at Södertälje's goalie, Curt Larsson, but he had also been tipped off about other players. He was told to go scout Brynäs, because Sweden's top team had some good, tough players. There might have been other tipsters too:

- Des Moroney, Sweden's B-team coach. Perhaps he said something to someone.
- Billy Harris, Tre Kronor's coach in 1972. He played twelve NHL seasons, most of them in Toronto. He had contacts in Canada.
- Bob Woods, a former curler who had a reputation for tipping off Canadian teams about Swedish players. Woods lived in Stockholm and ran one of the first hockey schools in Sweden. He watched the Swedish teams and had contacts in Canada.

So, when the Barrie Flyers, one of Canada's best amateur teams in 1972, travelled to Sweden to play a Christmas and New Year's tour, McNamara came too. We surprised them with hard hitting and fast skating. Stig and I played our normal game, refusing to back down and dishing out a few bruises when required. We angered the Canadians, who disliked losing to Swedish amateurs.

Our best player was Inge Hammarström. He scored four goals that night in a display that caught McNamara's eye.

Inge and I didn't really know what to believe after McNamara's visit. No one in Sweden seemed to understand how the NHL worked. All we had were plenty of rumors, nonsense, and fairy tales.

We didn't know if we were coming or going. The club bosses in Brynäs would certainly have been upset if I told them I was thinking of leaving. My hockey confidants were concerned that accepting a job in the NHL doomed a player to be treated solely as a commodity.

On TV and in the press, there was considerable debate about professionals and amateurs. Then, in the midst of all the discussion came word that a lawyer had begun to organize a sort of trade union for Swedish hockey players. He had a strange surname.

Wagnsson.

The players wondered what he was up to because it was also rumored that he had NHL contacts in the USA and Canada. In time I would come to know Björn Wagnsson both as a good businessman who was on the side of the players, and as a good and amusing friend.

But there were a few months left before we'd meet.

*   *   *

After our physical games against Team Canada, the rough play carried over into our own season. Maybe the Canadians had inadvertently made an impression on us. As well, Brynäs had become a target after three straight Swedish Gold Cups. We were no angels, but most of the rough play was initiated by teams that had decided we could be knocked off balance by dirty tactics.

Until the Christmas break we had barreled through the schedule like a freight train. We opened the season with six consecutive victories, outscoring our opponents 39-5. By Christmas, we had only lost one game.

But, as I said, we were being driven hard and every team fought like animals to upset the three-time champions. We were unable to maintain our pre-Christmas pace and ended up placing fourth, losing the Swedish Gold Cup to Leksand.

I played erratically that spring. My game was strong but I was spending too much time in the penalty box. I was second in the league in penalty time, after Ulf Sterner. Among other misdeeds, there was the incident with Finn Lundström in Timrå ("Today's hockey scandal," wrote one paper). But despite my hot-headedness I was still chosen to play for Sweden at the world championships.

First, though, I needed a lecture.

After playing a few exhibition games before the world championships, the skillful and popular coach Kjell Svensson called me into his office for a chat.

"You must calm down, Börje," he said. "It's good to play hard but sometimes you take needless penalties. No one can win games from the bench.

"You're too good a player to carry on like this."

It was no fun hearing it, but Kjell was right. I had to smarten up. To continue to copy the roughhousing Canadians would serve no useful purpose. Kjell was criticized for his world championship selections, but the criticism was unfair. Kjell was capable and had a knack for getting us to work together. He had a sense of humor, but he also commanded respect, and not just because he had been world champion in Colorado in 1962.

What I liked most about Kjell was his directness. He was upfront and honest with people. In addition he was one of the few coaches who talked to me seriously about the NHL.

5

Moscow
Cocktail

Soon after the team checked into the Ukraine Hotel in central Moscow, I learned Gerry McNamara was in the same hotel.

He wasn't alone. Other scouts and agents were milling about during the 1973 world championships, which quickly turned into a tournament of rumors, intrigue, and suspense.

The presence of representatives from professional clubs angered our management and they were understandably perturbed by the lobbying in the corridors. The Canadians tried to talk to me a few times, but the discussions went nowhere because of my broken English. They didn't press matters because I think they wanted to be as discreet as possible to placate our management.

Then there was this Wagnsson. He turned up in all sorts of places. Who was he anyway?

When I thought about it, I realized that it might be a good idea to retain a lawyer to handle my business affairs.

Wagnsson had informed both Inge and me that he would be happy to represent us in negotiations with the Maple Leafs. I decided to accept his offer.

The Swedish Embassy always organized receptions when the Swedish national team was in Moscow. This time, the reception came halfway through the tournament. Wagnsson showed up, of course (he seemed to be everywhere), and told some funny stories. But he also had a serious side. When we were alone, he asked how my negotiations were going.

"I don't know," I told him. "They certainly seem interested."

"Go slow and don't sell yourself too cheap," he said. "Remember, the NHL deals in big money."

"How big?" I wondered.

"Fifty to sixty thousand dollars. But I can check with Thommie Bergman and pull a few other strings. I definitely think you should play it cool and wait until after the tournament. I know McNamara and I know he is very interested in you. I'll help you if you like."

This type of negotiation was all new to me. On the one hand, why should an agent earn money from me? At the same time, I understood that he was considerably more skillful than I was at the art of making deals. I wasn't thinking only of the contract, but the entire question of moving to another country and the complications involved with taxation and other financial matters.

So I hired Wagnsson, which turned out to be one of the best decisions I've ever made. No one, not me or any of the other players, had any idea how to handle tough negotiations. How much was too much? How much was too little? How does a player determine how much he's really worth?

It's difficult to put a price on yourself or your services. At the same time, it's easy to be impressed by promises of expensive clothes and big cars. Professional sports is as much about extravagance and entertainment as about sport itself, especially in North America where there is big money to be made by the owners of hockey teams. Over the years, I have learned to handle my own affairs, but I always seek my lawyer's advice before I sign any contract. It is worth the cost.

Björn Wagnsson is honest and he's a nice guy. But I consult him because I need sound advice to protect me from being cheated. Some people believe sports lawyers are parasites and unscrupulous, and there are certainly some rotten eggs out there, but I trust Björn. I'd never undertake important business affairs without the help of an experienced and knowledgeable advisor.

*   *   *

A strange and exciting feeling permeated the 1973 world championships. It was no ordinary tournament. For the players dreaming of an NHL career, there was a lot at stake. Just being in Moscow heightened the anxiety; the whole city was full of shady deals. Glasnost has changed Moscow in recent years, but in 1973 it was a city dominated by the black market, vodka, and easy girls.

I was ignorant about the ways of the NHL. It wasn't until I moved to Toronto that I learned that there are few shady deals in North American hockey. There is a lot of money and high expectations, but agreements are strictly regulated and the contracts are clear-cut.

When I left Sweden, Swedish hockey was different. Players received money under the table, free cars, and other secret benefits. Now it seems better organized with standard contracts, salaries and, of course, taxes. During the early '70s, there was an intensive debate going on in hockey. One side argued that NHL professionals should be eligible for the world championships. But the Soviets and their eastern-block allies were adamantly opposed to an open competition, and they received the backing of the Swedish delegates to the International Ice Hockey Federation. Supposedly, they wanted to protect the integrity of amateur sport. What a joke! Everyone knew the Soviets were full-time hockey players, just like the NHL professionals. And everyone knew the Swedish players were paid—although the amounts were small.

It was plain hypocrisy, and young Anders Hedberg said as much at a press conference.

"We are all professionals, and everyone knows it," he said.

This inclination to bring professionalism out of the closet was worrisome to the Swedish Hockey Federation. Its members understood that an exodus of hockey talent was quickly approaching. That season, Thommie Bergman had signed with the Detroit Red Wings and all reports indicated that he'd done well. The federation felt pressed to do something before more players followed Bergman. So president Helge Berglund raised the allowance for Sweden's players at the world championship from 5,000 to 11,000 crowns ($700 to $1,575).

But it was too little, too late. The federation had lost touch with the real world. They were still kicking their ball around the defensive zone while the rest of the world had moved to the attack.

Bruce Norris, owner of the Red Wings, was associated with an established European professional league and had even signed a contract to play games in Gothenburg, Sweden. Attempts to also play in Stockholm were blocked by Berglund. The league never amounted to much, although its founding member, the London Lions, remained intact. It maintained an association with the Red Wings, becoming a kind of farm team for European players. Its team members included "Honken" Holmqvist, Tord Lundström, and Ulf Sterner—legendary Swedes.

*   *   *

After the cocktail party at Moscow's Swedish Embassy, Wagnsson handled all my negotiations with Toronto. I sat in on only one of the talks at the Ukraine Hotel. It came after Björn called my room and said the Leafs had requested a meeting with Inge Hammarström and me. So I slipped on my jacket and tie, part of the national team uniform, and put on my coolest expression.

The meeting was not particularly dramatic. It consisted mainly of polite talk to learn how much money we wanted.

"We don't want to distract you during the tournament," began McNamara, "but from what we've seen so far, we'd like you to come to Toronto and find out what we have to offer."

I don't remember our reply, but neither Inge nor I said much. Björn did the talking. He told them we were interested, but wouldn't be making a decision until after the tournament.

Together with Björn, we had been trying to decide how much money to demand for a two-year contract. Björn had investigated what Canadian players were making. He suggested I ask for $50,000.

So I was prepared when the question arose.

"How much do you want for two seasons?"

I was nervous.

"I don't know, about fifty or sixty thousand dollars a year," I answered clumsily. "I don't know exactly."

Björn broke in.

"We can leave the details until later," he said. "First they have to finish the tournament. Then we'll talk again."

After some more small talk, we left. Inge and I were unsure just what to make of the meeting, but Björn reassured us that it had gone well. "Relax," he said. "Everything's fine."

Sweden had opened the tournament by flattening Poland, 11-2, West Germany, 8-2, and then beating the reigning champions, Czechoslovakia, 2-0. Finland posed a problem, but Mats Åhlberg scored late in the game to give us a 3-2 win.

Coach Svensson used me frequently in all the games, and my play improved as the tournament went on. I was spurred on by the wonderful team spirit fostered by Svensson, and by the knowledge that Leaf scouts McNamara and Bob Davidson were watching my every move. I hadn't distinguished myself in the hotel room as a clever negotiator, but on the ice I could show them what I was worth.

The memorable but rough 1972 series between Canada and the Soviet Union seemed to set the tone for the world tournament seven months later. The game between Czechoslovakia and the Soviets was a complete scandal. Michailov ran over the Czech goalkeeper, Holecek, one of the many illegal tactics employed as the Soviets stopped a strong Czech team, 3-2. After the game, Czechoslovakia reported that eight players had been injured.

Their confidence at its peak, the Soviets then disposed of us easily, 6-1. They won the gold medal, outscoring

their opponents 100-18. We placed second, our goal dif-
ferential 53-23.

In crushing all opposition, the Soviets demonstrated
clearly that they were every bit as good and as professional
as the NHL. Sweden, on the other hand, was at best half
professional.

Our playoff match against Czechoslovakia was a struggle. We were losing 3-2 and Kjell had me play almost the
entire last period. It was tiring, but somehow the wetter
my shirt became, the better I played. As the minutes ticked
away, the Czech defence got tighter and tighter. Finally, old
Ulf Sterner woke up and scored to make it 3-3. I was glad
it was Ulf who got the goal. Sterner was the oldest and
most respected player on the team. His linemates were
Hedberg and Ulf Nilsson, two young speedsters with
whom Sterner liked to share a joke.

"I can't keep up with those kids," he'd say.

Now I'm in the same situation.

"So how does it feel, Uncle Salming?" said Sterner, pat-
ting me on the shoulder during a meeting at the 1989
world championships in Stockholm.

Sterner had an up-and-down game against the Czechs, but
his goal positioned us to win the silver medal—if we could
beat the Finns. Sure enough, as happens whenever Finland
plays Sweden, the Finns fought like crazy. Their goaltender,
Antti Leppänen, played like he was in a trance. The score
was 1-1 with only a few minutes left. Then it happened, the
play that to this day remains my sweetest hockey memory....

I get the puck in our own zone and look but no one's
open for a pass. So I carry the puck into the neutral
zone, cross the centre line and swing over to the right.
The whole time I'm looking to pass, but I can't find anyone open. A Finnish defender bumps me but I'm moving

fast and brush past him easily. Then I'm speeding over the blueline.

I look towards the front of the net and the defenceman thinks I'm ready to pass. He hesitates, trapped for a fraction of a second by his own indecision, and I know I have him. I accelerate in one final burst, and cut behind him. Then I'm upon the goal, alone with Leppänen, the puck on my stick, the expectation of all Sweden on my shoulders. And I score. There is no better feeling in sport than to fight hard for a whole game and then emerge as the hero. Nothing can match the pleasure of seeing ecstasy in the eyes of your teammates, hearing their shouts of joy and feeling their warm embrace. I just roared.

It's odd, but I don't remember exactly how I scored the goal. I remember being alone with Leppänen and then seeing the puck in the net. The rest I've learned from newspapers and television. There are so many split-second decisions and so many reflex reactions in hockey that it is impossible to remember them all. We have to let intuition guide us, and it guided me well that day against Finland.

Björn Wagnsson wore a delighted expression when I bumped into him later at the hotel. We both knew that my splendid goal would be a hot topic of discussion in the Maple Leafs' boardroom. His plan was to return to Sweden to chat with Thommie Bergman before beginning negotiations with Toronto.

"It'll work out," said Björn, poking a pinch of his ever-present tobacco under his lip.

I had decided to lie low and trust his judgment. He seemed to know what he was doing. Toronto's negotiators wanted the contract signed quickly, but Björn played it cool.

"Keep calm," he said. "We have all the aces."

Still, I was worried and a little impatient. They were talking about amounts I'd never dreamed of: $50,000 dollars a year, 350,000 crowns—staggering sums in 1973 for a 22-year-old hockey player. I wondered if we shouldn't conclude the deal as soon as possible, before they changed their minds.

On the plane home from Moscow, I staked out a seat near Coach Svensson. I trusted his judgment and felt comfortable discussing my future with him. He wasn't part of management, even though he was the federation captain. He always said what he believed, not what others expected him to say.

"So you're going professional," he said with a sideways grin.

"You never know," I replied. "Toronto's after me all right. What do you think?"

"You should go if you get the chance," he said. "It might not come again. Sweden will still be here if things go wrong."

These were the warmest and most encouraging words I ever heard from a federation official. And he spoke from experience. During his playing days as a goaltender, Svensson had attended a training camp in Toronto.

*   *   *

Back in Gävle I waited for Björn to phone. Other pro clubs had begun to express interest in me, although I don't know how much of it was genuine and how much was just rumors. Either way, I said a definite no to all who called. "Björn Wagnsson is taking care of my business. Call him," I'd say. Tommy Sandlin, Brynäs's coach, has said he was offered ten percent of my transfer fee plus ten percent of my future earnings, if he convinced me to sign with the Quebec Nordiques, who were then in the WHA. But Tommy never had time for shady business deals. As well, the Los Angeles Kings are supposed to have offered a hockey federation official 50,000 crowns if he could deliver me. Björn finally rang me in May.

"It's time. We're going to Toronto to conclude negotiations. You and Inge will be playing for them in the autumn."

But I was hesitant.

Björn had contract matters well in hand, and Inge was a fine travelling companion, but I had doubts because my English was poor. I felt alone. The solution came in Margitta Wendin. We had been together for only ten months, but if I was going to move to Canada she wanted to follow, and I wanted her by my side. Two days before our departure, I rang Björn.

"I want to bring Margitta."

He sounded unimpressed.

"What? Come on, Börje. We leave in two days. It'll be hard to arrange. You aren't even married."

"Tell them I'm not coming without her."

Björn laughed, but somehow he arranged an extra ticket. It was the first time I recognized Björn's talent for getting things done in a hurry. There would be other examples.

6

Big
Money

It was early June, 1973, when Margitta and I climbed
into Inge's blue BMW. As usual, it was spotlessly clean and
in a way it felt right. We were leaving for the most important and most lucrative negotiations of our young lives.

We drove south from Gävle to pick up Wagnsson who
was waiting for us at the Stockholm courthouse. From
there, Henning Sjöström provided a chauffeur-driven Rolls
Royce to take us to Bromma airport. We felt on top of the
world. We knew our position for the negotiations was
excellent. They wouldn't have invited us over if they didn't
plan to do everything they could to keep us.

Still, we had to stay calm, as tough as that was for a boy
from Kiruna who was impressed by Gävle, not to mention
Stockholm.

A big American car met us at the Toronto airport, and
McNamara invited us to sit in the back.

It all seemed unreal.

I kept wondering what Börje Salming was doing here. I told myself not to be impressed, that I was dealing with flesh and blood people just like me. The skyscrapers whizzed by and the gentlemen were very friendly. The Maple Leafs worked hard to win us over. During three days in Toronto, we visited Niagara Falls, saw a Roy Orbison and Chubby Checker concert, ate in fine restaurants, went shopping, and toured the city.

Team management was friendly, but they disapproved of Margitta tagging along. They smuggled us into a hotel near the airport under false names, which helped to keep reporters away. Margitta was introduced to the media as our interpreter. Unfortunately, she was an interpreter without a wardrobe. Her baggage had ended up in Rome. So she went shopping as soon as we arrived in Toronto.

Neither Margitta nor I cared how the Maple Leafs introduced us. We just wanted to get the deal finalized quickly.

Toronto is a beautiful city—clean, safe, friendly, cosmopolitan. We liked it immediately. But sightseeing wasn't what brought us there. We were lured by the twin opportunities of hockey and money.

The trans-Atlantic negotiations we had entered into were new to all parties. Players today move freely between countries and everyone understands clearly the relationships between players, agents, and management. The NHL Players' Association has standard player contracts, and young foreign players are subject to the annual NHL draft. But it was different in 1973; we were breaking new ground.

The upstart World Hockey Association, a rival professional league, added another confusing element to the mix. But one thing was clear: it was a player's market and anything was possible during negotiations. I didn't know it at the time, but I later learned that the value of a contract could range anywhere from $25,000 in the NHL up to the fairy-tale sum of $600,000 in the WHA.

On my second day in Toronto, I met with some Leaf players and ate with them at the Hot Stove Lounge in Maple Leaf Gardens. I also met the team owner, a controversial figure who dominated life at the Gardens, the late Harold Ballard.

At first, I formed no clear impression of him. Ballard left most of the talking to the club's general manager, Jim Gregory. After lunch, we adjourned to Gregory's office for contract talks.

We discussed a two-year deal, and the sums of $50,000 and $60,000 were mentioned. Björn spoke on my behalf, with Margitta translating. But we were having trouble reaching an agreement.

Finally, Gregory handed Inge and me a piece of paper from his desk.

"Write down how much you want," Gregory said.

We were reluctant, though, to commit ourselves without discussing our next move with Björn.

First, Björn took Inge into the corridor for a private consultation. While they were gone, Ballard and Gregory made small talk with Margitta and me. The atmosphere was strained. Then Inge returned and it was my turn to meet with Björn.

"What should I write?" I whispered. "Should we ask for $60,000?"

Björn seemed just as excited as Margitta and I were.

"Write $85,000," he said. "We can negotiate from there."

So I wrote $85,000. Gregory accepted the papers and read them, remaining expressionless. He looked up.

"I'm sure we can reach an agreement," he said.

More small talk followed and they agreed to give Björn their answer before we left for Sweden the next day.

* * *

When Margitta and I came down to breakfast the next morning, Björn looked pleased. Inge was also smiling.

"They gave us everything we asked for," blurted out Björn, who had just brought home his first professional deal.

I was delighted. I was making 1,000 crowns (about $143) per month with Brynäs. I'd make fifty times that amount with the Maple Leafs. No job for me in Sweden, in or out of hockey, could have paid me so handsomely. This contract was beyond even the wildest dreams of the boy from Kiruna.

Björn had one last card to play. He didn't sign any papers in Toronto. He wanted the deal finalized in Stockholm.

Inge had already started to dress for his new professional life. He liked style and smart clothes. When the national team was issued new shoes, Inge added some money of his own and bought a particularly smart pair, which he wore to Toronto.

On the way home, Björn decided to celebrate our success with one of his many practical jokes. When Inge took off his shoes and fell asleep on the plane, Björn snatched one shoe and put it in Margitta's handbag. We had a good laugh when the plane landed in Copenhagen and Inge, helped by a stewardess, crawled the length of the plane in search of his lost shoe.

Inge finally limped from the plane to join me alongside the TV crew that was waiting to interview us about our professional deal, which was big news at home. Though embarrassed, Inge kept a straight face. Luckily, the camera crew never shot below the waist.

We wanted to give Brynäs a chance to talk to the Toronto management, which was one reason for asking them to come to Stockholm. Björn knew that there would be more deals in the future, and he was eager to soften the blow to the Swedish clubs as best he could. But it was no easy task. Inge and I felt a bit like traitors and wanted to give the Brynäs management a chance to seek some sort of settlement with the Maple Leafs.

We saw the Toronto contract as our reward of money and adventure for all our hours of hard training. But Thure Wickberg and Henry Jansson were upset by the signing. I understood their position. They had dedicated their lives to Brynäs and they were hurt that a couple of young players would abandon the club just when they could help it the most.

Thure vented his anger by freezing our allowance from the world championships. The Federation was responsible for writing the cheques, but the clubs were entrusted with distributing the money to the players.

"It only goes to players who are coming back next season," said Thure. We didn't want to make a fuss, so we kissed the money goodbye.

We also didn't complain when we were forced to leave the A-team dressing room during summer training with Brynäs. We had to move into a small, nearby room. Some people have said that we were thrown out, but that's not entirely true. Our places were simply given to our replacements. It was no big deal. Inge and I were planning to turn professional, and Brynäs management was doing its best to prepare for the coming season.

Jim Gregory arrived in Stockholm in the middle of June and checked into the Sheraton Hotel. Wickberg and Jansson chose the Carlton a couple blocks away. Inge and I waited in Gävle for a message from Wagnsson. The time dragged.

Although Inge and I had reached an agreement with the Maple Leafs, Toronto and Brynäs still had to settle on a transfer fee that would satisfy Brynäs. We had no idea how much Brynäs would demand or how high the Maple Leafs would go to buy us.

All we knew was that Wickberg and Jansson were not in a conciliatory mood. Their opening demand hit like a punch in the gut.

Björn Wagnsson tells it like this:

After Gregory met Wickberg and Jansson at the Carlton, he went to Wagnsson's office. He looked glum.

"This won't work, Björn," Gregory said. "They're asking for $60,000. I can't give them that kind of money."

"I have an idea," said Wagnsson. "Thure Wickberg has a son, a good player on the national team. Suggest that Toronto is thinking of buying another Swede next year, maybe a national player, possibly even someone named Wickberg."

Gregory returned to the Carlton and soon a deal was struck. A few days later, I got a call from Björn.

"It's time to sign. Everything is ready."

Once more we drove to Stockholm in Inge's BMW. Björn showed us the contract, which we had already seen. Our signing in the courthouse cellar was more or less a formality.

Afterwards, we were invited to Henning Sjöström's Archipelago villa at Skärvsta outside Stockholm. Sjöström was Björn's employer and he extended the same hospitality to Gregory that Gregory had shown us in Toronto. I had found a job.

7

Blood, Sweat and Fools

Inge and I arrived in the NHL when the game was at its violent worst. Hockey was growing and developing around the world, but in the NHL it was being strangled in the unenlightened hands of some backwards-thinking men.

NHL expansion, coupled with the birth of the WHA, caused the number of big-league jobs to swell from a level of about 100 in 1967 to more than 500 by our arrival in 1973. This rapid growth had a negative impact on the quality of the game.

Players' salaries doubled and tripled, but the calibre of play declined for several years. There just weren't enough good players to go around. There was, however, a seemingly endless supply of fighters, which resulted in scandalous brawling during the mid-'70s, occasionally involving even the police and the public.

In Sweden, I was seen by many as a fighter. In North America, I played the same style but I was a pussycat compared to the beasts of the NHL.

I was taken aback on my first day at training camp to see one fat, toothless Maple Leaf after another stroll into the dressing room. Few of them looked like hockey players, at least not like top Swedish players. The worst was a toothless giant with the biggest feet I'd ever seen who plodded into the rookies' room. I took one look at him and wondered if all the horror stories we'd heard back in Sweden were true.

"What have I gotten myself into?" I thought, but it wasn't the time to say much.

All players, both young and old, looked tough. The rotund giant with the big feet was Bob Neely, a first-round draft pick who came from junior hockey with a reputation for brawling. His hockey skills were nothing special, but he could fight. One rumor had it that he'd played for a time with his arm in a plaster cast, which he used to deliver punishing forearm smashes.

Neely's style was typical of the hockey popular in the NHL when I arrived. Slashing, elbowing, and fighting were considered normal. But even Neely was overwhelmed by the violence. He was regarded as one of the toughest players in junior hockey, but after a few NHL games, even he was less inclined to fight.

Inge and I arrived in top physical condition. We'd worked out all summer to get our bodies rock-hard for whatever rigors awaited us. With those tough exhibition games against Canadian teams fresh in our minds, we had decided to leave nothing to chance. We had even skated for several weeks with Brynäs before climbing aboard the plane.

Our intense preparations paid immediate dividends.

We easily outskated the overweight Canadians. At that time, we didn't know that most NHL players reported to camp in poor condition and worked themselves into shape.

They labored through practice sessions in tights, sweating off excess pounds. It would be several more years before they caught up with European conditioning methods. Meantime, these flabby professionals, full-grown men skating in circles to sweat away their fat, looked ridiculous.

It's different today. Players are expected to report in good shape, and they're given individual training programs for the off-season. When they report to camp, they're weighed and scientifically tested to ensure they've attained a high level of fitness.

There were about 40 players at my first training camp. One after another, the numbers thinned as players were sent to the minor leagues. But Inge and I remained. I needed only one practice to realize I had a good shot at making the team. After a few weeks, I was sure we'd both make it.

The hockey went well for us. Toronto had a new coach, Red Kelly, and many new players. We weren't the only ones trying to find our way. Language was a problem, but I understood the hockey terminology. Besides, we weren't there to gab; we were there to play. Our teammates seemed to appreciate what we could do on the ice, which helped us feel accepted.

We also made it through the tough initiation that all NHL rookies must endure. It's not pleasant for anyone, but even worse for a rookie who is a bit cocky. Ian Turnbull, a skilled defenceman, arrived at the same time as me and was quickly brought down to earth after a few arrogant comments. After one exhibition game, a pair of the older guys snuck up on Ian and carted him off to the massage table in the middle of the dressing room. He screamed and squirmed like a snake, but to no avail. They tied him down, then shaved his head. That shut him up for a couple of days.

The exhibition games went smoothly. Inge led the team in scoring and, as the days passed, the players made us feel like part of the team. I had worried beforehand that we might be given the cold shoulder because, in some eyes, we were foreigners taking jobs from Canadians. But that attitude never became a serious problem.

My biggest worry during training camp was the back pain I developed after the first couple of practices. Athletes sometimes complain of mysterious backaches if they're looking to escape a high-pressure situation. When the pain began, I worried that some players might decide I was scared.

But Jim Gregory was understanding and arranged for George Armstrong, a former Toronto captain, to drive me to a chiropractor named John Neal. I was in some pain, but nonetheless Armstrong took a detour. He knew how young hockey players liked to spend some of their new wealth. We stopped at some car dealerships.

"Have you thought about what about kind of car you want?" he laughed, while introducing me to the salesmen.

I later bought a Camaro Z28, a young man's dream car. It cost about $3,500 and had 455 horse power. It was fantastic, like nothing I'd ever owned before. Heck, I used to inherit my brother's old bikes. I hardly ever drove a car in Sweden. Suddenly I was driving a brand new Z28.

But the novelty soon wore off. With the arrival of a family, my dream car didn't seem so dreamy any more.

After strolling through the showrooms with Armstrong, we proceeded to Dr. Neal's office. He turned out to be as good as Gregory promised. He treated me and gave me a corset, which I wore throughout my rookie season. I visited Dr. Neal often during my early years. My problems were related to the vertebrae I'd damaged when I fell from a fence while serving in the army. Dr. Neal did a great job. Without him, I could never have played.

During my years in the NHL, I realized over and over how tough it is to be a newcomer. It was fortunate that Inge and I had prepared ourselves so thoroughly. It's not only tough on the ice, but off of it as well. One minute you are confronting a screaming opponent, the next you're dealing with an obnoxious teammate. A rookie's day can be turned into hell if he makes the mistake of rubbing some dumb teammate the wrong way.

Some idiots delight in trying to intimidate rookies by staring them down or generally treating them like dirt. The only way to combat fools, opponents and teammates alike, is to ignore them and show them on the ice that you can't be intimidated.

A cocky newcomer often finds himself being demoted to the farm team largely because a brash rookie has problems making friends. Without the support and encouragement of friends, it's tough to survive in the NHL. It's best for a new player to stay quietly in the background. In time you'll be accepted and given the chance to show what you can do on the ice.

Most veterans are decent men and remember how it felt to be new. They don't want to hurt anyone, but they're not likely to help a rookie who is loud, arrogant, and continually making a fool of himself. That type of player doesn't usually last long in the league.

I started out by keeping a low profile. I didn't say much, largely because I had little confidence in my English. But it turned out that my quiet demeanor helped me get my first permanent stall in the dressing room. The guy who sat next to team captain Dave Keon got sent to the minors, leaving a spot vacant. Keon didn't like a lot of talking when he got dressed for games. He liked it calm and quiet. So he told trainer Guy Kinnear, "Put Salming here."

No one asked my opinion. I just collected my gear and moved. It meant I was accepted.

As my NHL debut neared, I was nervous. Our exhibition schedule showed Inge and me that we were good enough for the NHL. But, still, on opening night I had the jitters. The Swedish ambassador, Åke Malmaeus, stopped by before the game to wish us luck. The atmosphere was tense.

But the game went much better than expected.

We played the Buffalo Sabres in front of the standard sell-out crowd at Maple Leaf Gardens, about 16,500. I was teamed on defence with Ian Turnbull and we both played well in a 7-4 victory. The public and the press accepted me with open arms. In fact, I was named the game's first star.

The award was a surprise, because my back ached and I didn't feel like I'd done anything special. I'd only played my normal game, throwing bodychecks, moving the puck quickly to the forwards, and skating as usual. By Canadian standards, I skated well, especially for a defenceman.

Jim Proudfoot, writing in the *Toronto Star*, commented on how I threw myself in front of a shot with just 10 seconds left in the game and the score 7-4. "He's just what the Leafs need," Proudfoot wrote.

Everything was going to be all right. Inge and I measured up. But with the debut over, the real test would come two days later. We were off to Philadelphia to play the Flyers.

Reports about the Leafs' new Swedish players preceded us to Philadelphia. The Flyers were feared and renowned throughout the NHL. They didn't have just a couple of ruffians, they had twenty! They played a violent style, fighting at the drop of an insult, and they were successful. No team was tougher or more intimidating. The Flyers were the undisputed heavyweight champions of the NHL—and they didn't take kindly to rookies from Sweden.

The Flyers of that era were a gang of butchers. They used fear like a seventh man on the ice. And it worked. Visiting players suddenly became ill before games in the Spectrum. Around the league the illness was known as the Phillie flu.

"You're dead meat, chicken-Swede!"

That was the type of welcome I got in Philadelphia, from both the Flyers and their fans.

"Kill them! Kill them! Kill them! Kill them!" chanted the crowd.

But thanks to years of colliding with my brother, and thanks to run-ins with Finn Lundström, and thanks to all the taunting I heard in rinks across Sweden, I wasn't really worried. It was unpleasant and a bit unsettling, but not frightening. Actually, I was hyped up. I decided that rather than avoid trouble, I'd do just the opposite: I'd hit back.

It didn't take long.

Early in the first period, we lined up for a face-off in our end. The Flyer players taunted me while their biggest goon, left winger Dave (Hammer) Schultz, stared at me. The puck went into the corner and Schultz and I chased it. We collided. The puck went around the boards, but Schultz didn't follow. He turned and slashed me hard with his stick. I hit him back. Schultz stared at me, his eyes blazing like a madman's. It was humiliating for him to be struck so brazenly by a rookie. Then he slashed me across the chest. I hit him right back, hard, and winded him. A general free-for-all was soon under way. My personal battle with Schultz ended in a draw, but for me it was a clear victory.

I showed that I wasn't going to be anybody's punching bag, and if necessary I would give as good as I got. I also knew that I had won the full respect of my teammates when they rushed to my defence after the Schultz attack.

Throughout the years I was involved in other brawls (they're almost unavoidable in the NHL), but not too many. Sometimes it's necessary to stand up and fight. If you don't, you'll only be pestered by loudmouths whose sole function is to intimidate and fight.

The most scandalous brawl I ever witnessed was against the same Flyers during the 1976 playoffs.

By that time, fighting in the league had become epidemic. There were widespread demands from people inside and outside of hockey for a crackdown. They wanted the game returned to the stylists. Finally, after a brutal playoff game in the Gardens, the issue found its way to a Toronto court.

Unfortunately I was involved, both as a combatant and as a witness at an assault trial.

The incident began when Schultz and Tiger Williams got into a fight. Soon, a full-scale brawl erupted. I was paired off with Flyers' centre Mel Bridgman. But other Flyers players held on to me and as they restrained me Bridgman let me have it.

Fans began throwing debris, including eggs and golf balls, and in the chaos players and spectators were hitting each other. It's hard to say exactly what happened but, without a doubt, the situation was out of control.

Assault charges were laid against Bob "Mad Dog" Kelly, Don Saleski, Joe Watson, and Bridgman, all of them Flyers. Kelly had thrown a glove from the penalty box that had inadvertently struck a woman. Watson was accused of using a dangerous weapon (his stick) to clip a policeman during the uproar.

The case came to trial in the summer, and it was an unpleasant experience for everyone involved from both teams. Most of us felt the matter didn't belong in court. It should have been handled internally by the NHL. We all felt ashamed to be in court.

I was called as a witness. My intention was to explain exactly what happened, but I never got the chance. I'd never been at a trial before, so I was easy prey for the lawyer representing the Philadelphia players. I tried calmly to describe what had happened, but he kept firing provocative questions at me.

"Isn't it true that fighting is part of the game?"

"Yes, but ..."

"Don't you usually trade insults with the opposition?"

"No, it's only ..."

"So what happened was completely normal?"

"Normal ... It wasn't really ..."

"Nothing unusual, anyway."

He interrupted me continually, and it was clear I should have brought an interpreter. My English was fundamentally sound but the right words became difficult to find amid the pressure and badgering. The case didn't matter to me personally. I was only a witness. My noble intention was simply to help uncover the truth. When that appeared impossible, I basically gave up and answered yes to all his questions.

Yes.

Yes.

Yes.

It wasn't worth saying anything else.

I believe that the Flyers players received no more than small fines.

The trial was unimportant to me because my revenge had been exacted during the game. Following the fight with Bridgman, Darryl Sittler hit me with a perfect break-away pass and I scored on goalie Bernie Parent. Somehow it felt as if I had shown Bridgman. It is one of the few goals I remember clearly, partly because of the standing ovation I received from the wonderful Toronto supporters.

The NHL has less fighting now than during those dreadful days when the Flyers terrorized the league. The rules were changed so that the third man into a fight is automatically ejected from the game. There are also severe penalties to coaches and teams that participate in bench-clearing brawls. Fighting still remains, but mostly one-on-ones rather than the wild free-for-alls common during the 1970s.

Back then, full-scale brawls were frequent, and I can vouch for the authenticity of the blows. It wasn't like professional wrestling, with a few fake slaps and play-acting. It was punches in the face until blood ran. Quite literally, many players were forced to fight to stay in the league.

Our policeman in Toronto was a tough left winger named Dave Williams, although few would remember him by that name. He was known as Tiger. He played 14 seasons in the NHL for the Maple Leafs, Vancouver Canucks, Detroit Red Wings, Los Angeles Kings, and Hartford Whalers.

I first met Tiger when I arrived at training camp in my second season. Walking into the Gardens, I noticed an odd character in front of me with boxing gloves dangling from his shoulders. I next saw him in the dressing room, and he was still carrying the gloves.

We certainly needed him. During the '70s, successful teams needed one or two good fighters, if only for self-defence. Tiger was a master at his craft. And he wasn't a bad hockey player.

He was fun to watch in a fight. He wasn't the biggest or the strongest fighter in the league, but he had more guts and heart than any fighter I've known. He'd get knocked down and, even if a couple of players tried to pin him, he'd struggle back to his feet, shake himself off, and continue the battle.

Tiger was a fighter in many ways. When he first joined us in the 1974-75 season, he was a poor skater. But he persevered and stayed after practice for extra skating drills. He took power-skating lessons and even dabbled in figure skating to improve his balance.

While I confronted trouble head-on, Inge used the reverse tactic when faced with NHL violence. He sailed into corners at full speed and sailed out neatly and stylishly. He simply skated away from anyone who was chasing him, which angered his foes and earned Inge the reputation of being a coward.

Inge was not a coward. His style was just unsuited to the NHL at that time. He didn't want to fight. But the Flyers set the tone and their violent ways were adopted across the league.

Eventually, the pendulum swung back to the swift, precision skating of Montreal and Edmonton. The Canadiens were a skillful team who won four consecutive Stanley Cups (1976-79). They combined the speed and playmaking of European hockey with traditional North American toughness. It was a compromise of styles that I admired.

After the Canadiens' style became the vogue, it was amusing to watch the Philadelphia gang of hooligans being disbanded and dispersed around the league. Many of them were scared stiff. They were tough and intimidating when travelling in a pack, but on their own they proved to be small, nervous men.

I remember playing against the Pittsburgh Penguins in 1979. One of their players had been a bully in Philadelphia, but he looked terrified when my friend and defence partner Dave Hutchison hissed, "You're not so tough now. This isn't Philadelphia any more. We're gonna get you."

Several Flyers players quit hockey soon after being traded from Philadelphia.

When the Canadiens dethroned the Flyers in 1976, it was a victory for all of hockey. But unfortunately it was too late for Inge.

He was the right man at the wrong time, especially in Toronto. By 1977 we had a promising young team that seemed headed for the Stanley Cup final. But a series of poor management decisions transformed us into a mediocre club that eventually would struggle just to make the playoffs.

Today, there is less emphasis on running into opponents. The primary focus is on skating and playmaking and, when it arises, coping with clean bodychecks. Few players feel that they have to fight.

I am convinced that Inge would have been a big star if he had come to the NHL ten years later. His style of skating and playmaking was perfectly suited to the faster, more artistic game of the 1980s.

I'm not suggesting that Inge's years in the NHL were unsuccessful. On the contrary, he had six good seasons in the league (four in Toronto and two in St. Louis). He scored over a hundred goals for Toronto and for a time played on a deadly line with Lanny McDonald and Darryl Sittler.

Yet his stylish approach was never fully appreciated by his coaches. The astute hockey fans of Toronto enjoyed Inge's skillful stickhandling and skating, but club management, especially owner Harold Ballard, cringed when Inge avoided physical contact.

Ballard, who revelled in making outrageous public comments, once said about Inge:

"He could skate into a corner with six eggs in his pocket and not break any of them."

It was an unfair insult.

Ballard had forgotten Inge's two game-winning goals during the playoffs in our first season in Toronto. In the first round of a best-of-three series against Los Angeles, we lost Game 1, 3-2. We needed to win the next two games or be eliminated. With Inge scoring the deciding goals both nights, we won 3-2 and 2-1.

Inge also had trouble adjusting to the lifestyle away from the rink. He didn't drink and disliked it when the guys went out for a beer. Actually, in the seventies, it was seldom just one beer. We'd often carry on half the night.

I understand Inge. He had seen close up how alcohol abuse could ruin a life. He was always very careful and probably thought we were being juvenile. Inge recognized that in the NHL, where pressure and expectations are high, players were at greater risk. Many players are unable to cope with the setbacks that all players occasionally endure. For some, the problem is coping with success and hero worship.

I remember some players whose lives were overrun by alcohol, big, strong athletes who sought comfort in the bottle after a serious injury or a prolonged slump. The surest way to guard against the dangers of drink is to abstain, as Inge did, even at the risk of being called boring.

Travelling during the wild seventies, there were few quiet nights in the team hotel. I remember bowling with hotel lamps set up like pins, and watching a teammate empty a bottle of whiskey in his boot, drink it all, and declare "Fuck the world!"

He later collapsed with his clothes on.

After six NHL seasons, Inge returned to Gävle, played for Brynäs for a couple of years, and is now established comfortably in his own business. The NHL has also settled down.

Players are tamer now. There are still parties, but they're not as often or as raucous as in the seventies, when Inge and I arrived. The game is calmer, too. The quality of play and players has risen considerably. Expectations are also higher. A player who drinks and plays the fool will eventually find himself sipping alone from the cup of failure.

8

The Early Years

Our first year in the NHL was relatively trouble free. Maybe that was partly due to all the myths—and, for that matter, some truths—we'd heard about North American hockey. We came expecting the worst and found out that the NHL wasn't as bad as has been reported back home.

Inge and I took it in stride when players were demoted or traded, and we grew accustomed to the fighting. It was important to follow club rules and keep quiet.

We were expected to play hockey and stay at arm's length from club matters. It was different than what we were used to at home, but we had been cut from the tough hide of Brynäs and were prepared for surprises. It was a good time. We were popular and the team played well. In the beginning, Inge, Margitta, and I lived in the Westbury Hotel near Maple Leaf Gardens, a practical arrangement because we didn't know how long we would be staying.

But once the season was underway, Inge and I knew that we'd made the team. So Margitta and I found a four-room apartment outside the city, while Inge, a bachelor, found a small apartment downtown. My back acted up frequently, but I tried not to let it show. Dr. Neal's corset was a big help.

I found the travelling tiring, particularly the west-coast trips, during which we'd play four games in a week. Five or six hours on a plane was hard on my back and the three-hour time difference contributed to overall fatigue. But despite everything, I don't remember the early days as tough. Everything was so new and exciting, and I felt a strong sense of satisfaction at being able to support myself as a hockey player. It was just good fun. Presumably, I was also hardened by all the bus trips with Kiruna AIF at home in Norrbotten.

The Maple Leafs had experienced some dark years in the late sixties and early seventies. There was a corporate battle for control of the club—a fight that neither Inge nor I understood—that left Harold Ballard the winner. All of Toronto wanted to see the Leafs restored to their past glory, so in the mid-seventies, several new players were acquired.

They had a new coach, Red Kelly, which worked out well for us. Kelly had played on four Stanley Cup champions with the Leafs in the 1960s. Before accepting the Leaf coaching job, he'd coached the Pittsburgh Penguins for four years.

Inge and I supported each other, but there was one player on the team who really took care of us, Jim McKenny.

McKenny was a funny man, always ready with a quip and a smile. He had a big heart and was forever looking out for the new guys on the team. He made sure that the young rookies from Sweden were never left out of team activities.

After a few games and several practices, I felt as much at home at the Gardens as on the ice in Gävle. I was lucky that everything went well from the beginning and that I was playing well in the games. The guys understood that I was happy, even if I didn't say much.

While Inge and I made an easy adjustment, the NHL itself was having a tougher time learning to live with its rival, the World Hockey Association. The new pirate league was determined to establish itself in the USA and Canada. To gain instant credibility, WHA teams offered incredible contracts to entice NHL players to change leagues. Many players took the money and moved, but Inge and I, happy in Toronto and content with our salaries, didn't jump at the first attractive offers that came along.

During those tumultuous days, there was a lot of sneaking about in corridors as agents and lawyers listened to offers and negotiated contracts. Ballard lost fifteen to twenty players from the Leafs, his farm team, and the junior Marlboros during the WHA's early years. These were years in which the Philadelphia Flyers and Boston Bruins brawled best and won most. Canadians, accustomed to the traditional success of the Maple Leafs and the Montreal Canadiens, envied the achievements of the American-based teams. In Montreal and Toronto, fans and the media united to demand that the Stanley Cup be returned to Canada.

In Toronto, Kelly and the rest of us just wanted to play hockey. I soon became fed up with the never-ending tackles, punching, and dirty tricks, not to mention the foul language.

"You're dead, asshole!"

"I'm gonna kill you, motherfucker!"

"I'm gonna kick your balls out!"

Measured beside the goings-on in the NHL, the hockey we played in Sweden was kid's stuff. I was certainly no angel in Sweden, but any anger I vented was like shadow boxing compared to the bloody violence of the NHL. Some days it was like a parody of sport.

The challenge for me was to play as fairly and well as possible and not to sink to the shameful level of the thugs. Toronto's knowledgeable fans preferred a skillful play to an overhand right, and they supported me with fantastic ovations.

We made the playoffs in my first year with a record of 35 wins, 27 losses, and 16 ties. We had improved by 16 points over the previous season, and management seemed satisfied, even though we were knocked out in the first playoff round by the Boston Bruins, eventual finalists. Although we lost the best-of-seven playoff 4-0, the games were all close.

We lost by scores of 1-0, 6-3, 6-3, and 4-3, but every game was tight until the dying minutes. They would have all been one-goal losses if not for late goals scored into our open net after Kelly removed our goalie, Doug Favell, in a last-ditch attempt for a tie.

I was unhappy to lose, but nevertheless I was satisfied with my first season on the ice in the NHL. Both Inge and I had performed well under pressure and managed to play our own game.

What I found more difficult, however, was all the fuss off the ice. I often refused media interviews. I was uncomfortable answering questions, unsure of my English and worried that I'd say the wrong thing. At the same time, I felt like I was letting down the team. Players are expected to cooperate with the media and foster a good public image for the club. I was trapped in a no-win situation. I felt uncomfortable if I talked and uncomfortable if I didn't.

When my rookie season ended, I was voted the Molson Cup Maple Leafs' player of the year, which brought a $1,500 bonus. But this unexpected reward was followed by demands for me to attend banquets, give away prizes, make speeches, and accept invitations to dinner parties. I'd almost have preferred to meet one of Dave Schultz's elbows. I disliked the public demands that went with the job. When I was chosen for the all-star team in February, the Leafs had refused to release me because they feared I might be injured. I was almost relieved that I didn't have to go.

Once the season ended, Margitta and I travelled to our summer cottage outside Axmarby, near Gävle. It was great to escape the limelight, to return home and be able to do whatever I wanted without feeling the pressure of the next game or having a reporter ask questions. I could stay up as late as I wanted and sleep in as late as I liked.

My first year in Toronto was satisfying. Margitta and I decided to stay with the NHL for a couple more years. The hockey didn't feel too demanding and I enjoyed Toronto. We decided to buy a house in Mississauga, a suburb about twenty miles from the Gardens.

I spent my summer puttering around the cottage, building a wall on the patio, and planning for a future in Toronto. Our goal was to start a family and build a solid financial foundation before moving back to Sweden. There seemed no reason why I couldn't manage several more seasons in the NHL, even if there was a risk that I might someday be traded or sent down to the minors.

Actually I wasn't too worried. I knew my strengths and understood that as long as I kept fit, I'd be all right. In addition, the Leafs seemed to be heading towards a good future. I hoped that someday I'd be involved in a serious challenge for the Stanley Cup.

Behind the scenes, the NHL was in a state of flux. The existence of the WHA resulted in feverish competition for players, and salaries zoomed skyward. For the players, the bidding wars were great.

In 1966, the average NHL salary was $18,000. In 1972, it was $40,000. In 1976, after four years of WHA competition, the average wage had more than doubled to $90,000. In a single decade, salaries had increased five-fold.

Margitta and I pleased Toronto's management by getting married. Today, public attitudes in Canada are more liberal, but in 1973 people were puzzled when we said we weren't married. In Sweden, no one gave it a second thought.

The 1974-75 season opened with considerable optimism in Toronto, but, instead of building on our 86 points of the previous year, we slipped back to 78 points and were swept 4-0 in the playoffs by the Flyers, the eventual Stanley Cup champions. But we rebounded with a strong season the following year. It was about that time that the "Ballard Circus" hit town.

Harold Ballard revelled in the limelight. He loved to be loud and outrageous, the centre of attention wherever he went. His off-the-cuff comments frequently made headlines, but often left the players feeling like pieces in a board game manipulated at Ballard's will. The reporters loved Ballard's bluster. Overlooked, however, was the confusion and anxiety his statements caused in the dressing room. He was unpredictable and volatile, two traits that run contrary to the development of a stable, winning organization.

This unfortunate trend dated back to the latter part of the 1970s and continued until Ballard's death in 1990. (See Chapter 14, "Ballard and Me.").

There was a lot of talk in Toronto about the WHA. Before the '74-75 season, Paul Henderson jumped from the Leafs to the Toronto Toros, improving his salary from $90,000 to $140,000. Henderson wanted me to go with him.

"Hell, Börje, you should make some money, too," said Henderson.

The NHL owners were certainly worried, even though most players remained loyal to the NHL. The established league was still regarded as the best place to play professional hockey and many players opted for NHL prestige over WHA dollars.

So the '74-75 season got off to an uncertain start, and the mood wasn't improved when the Toronto papers wrote some true articles about the loud behavior of some players on a road trip. They had been drunk and a bit noisy on a plane, where of course everything is seen. At the same time, Ballard complained about Kelly and some of the players to the media. He wanted to see a harder line and more discipline.

The atmosphere in the dressing room, so upbeat in my rookie year, sank noticeably. But I tried not to worry about the unrest. When my contract with the Leafs expired at the end of the season, the Toros sent out feelers to discover if I'd jump to the WHA. The Toros were prepared to give me a big raise and a five-year deal. They also talked about signing Stig from Brynäs.

The Toros' coach was Billy Harris, whom I knew from his days as the coach of the Swedish national team. Wagnsson handled the negotiations, although I made it clear that I wasn't particularly interested in the Toros. I felt loyal to the Maple Leafs and wanted to do well there, and I also had little faith in the WHA. Clubs seemed to be constantly moving or folding. Players were bounced around. It was difficult to picture a day when the league would be stable.

It wasn't that the WHA was totally without appeal. Some players earned amazing salaries (as much as $600,000 a year, according to some accounts), but I was willing to make do with less money in exchange for a more stable lifestyle. Anders, our first son, had just been born, so I was reluctant to go off chasing rainbows.

"Calm down. You're in a great negotiating position," said Wagnsson, who was also exploring opportunities for Stig.

"Don't sign unless you get a good one-way contract," I advised my brother.

But the Toros offered Stig a two-way contract, which meant his salary would be greatly reduced if he was sent to the minors.

Stig was smart to decline the offer. He had just built a house and had a young family. I wouldn't recommend that anyone jump at a professional career unless his salary is guaranteed. Even then, it would have to be a good contract that paid well and allowed the family to settle in one place.

As it is, during the NHL season, family and social lives are practically non-existent because of the busy schedule and travel. That's why my summer vacations in Sweden are sacred. I seldom appear at banquets or charity functions, and have even occasionally neglected friends and relations. I devote those four months to my family. We need the time together.

My conscience suffers during the winter because of the time I'm separated from my family, so the long summers together with Margitta, Teresa and Anders are important. I sometimes think that the uninterrupted weeks work out better than if I had a job where I could manage only one or two hours each evening with my children.

Anyway, I stayed with the Maple Leafs. Wagnsson negotiated a five-year contract worth $170,000 annually. It was far more attractive than the prospect of possibly having to drift with an unstable WHA team, even if the money would have been better initially.

On to the
Stanley Cup

The three years leading up to the 1976 Canada Cup were the most fulfilling of my NHL career. Not only did hockey go well, but Margitta gave birth to Anders in 1974 and two years later to Teresa.

My life was perfect.

Everything had happened so fast since my 1973 debut against Buffalo. I'd made the NHL second all-star team twice, was popular in Toronto, was constantly approached for interviews or public appearances, got married, bought a house in Mississauga, and had two children. Each summer, we'd pack up and head back to Sweden for four glorious months.

There were no clouds on the horizon.

On the ice, Jim Gregory and Red Kelly had laid the foundation for a winning team. The Maple Leafs had a good blend of players with speed, skill, savvy, strength, and determination. Despite Harold Ballard's disruptive public statements, Darryl Sittler succeeded in building team spirit and enthusiasm. He was a perfect team captain, talented and respected as a player, and most of all a great leader off the ice.

"Okay, boys, everybody to the restaurant," he'd holler after practice, and everyone went because Sittler had an infectious, easy, and positive manner.

After road games, it is important for team spirit that the team stay together, killing the hours before it's time to sleep or catch a plane. When individuals go their own way, moaning and gossip usually follow. Cliques can develop, which inevitably lead to pockets of resentment and envy that destroy team morale.

Darryl's leadership was our safeguard. He kept us together.

Through the mid-seventies, our teams were young and hungry: Ian Turnbull, Darryl Sittler, Lanny McDonald, Tiger Williams, Pat Boutette, Ron Ellis, Georg Ferguson, Jim McKenny, Wayne Thomas, Doug Favell, Inge Hammarström, Paul Henderson, Brian Glennie, Errol Thompson, and, later, Mike Palmateer and Dave Hutchison. We believed that the Maple Leafs were on the way to being great again, building the foundation that would reclaim the Stanley Cup, last won by Toronto in 1967.

Our coach, Red Kelly, was an ordinary Canadian coach of the old school, but he cared about the players and he was patient. He was popular but perhaps too kind-hearted to coach young, ambitious hockey professionals. Kelly knew the game well enough. His problem was in getting us to play tough, consistent hockey, the style that wins Stanley Cups.

We were too meek and it hurt us in the playoffs.

In 1975 Philadelphia eliminated us in four games. The following year, we met the same gang of butchers in the quarter-finals. We believed we were ready for them.

1. My mother Karin holding me, her mother, Stig, and my father Erland. (above)

2. My mother and father practising gymnastics. (left)

3. My favorite hobby was to go fishing in Torne Lake. (opposite page)

4. This photo, taken before my time, shows the village of Salmi where my grandfather settled as a tradesman and took the name Salming. I spent many summers there. (above)

5. "Stigge" and I proudly showing off the day's catch, although we weren't so delighted about the berries. But we had to pick a bag of berries before we were allowed to fish. (left)

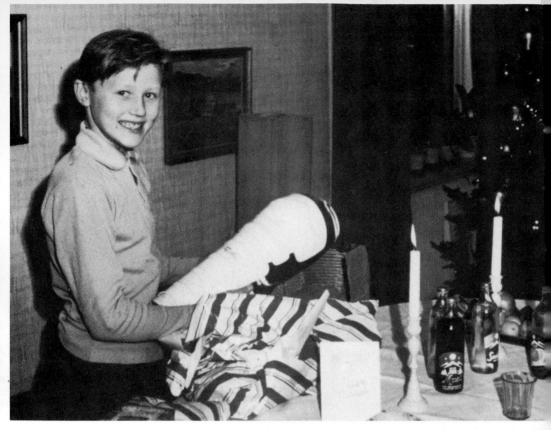

6. Could there be a better Christmas present! (above)

7. It was great to be able to do something for Kiruna AIF and all their wonderful junior coaches after Christmas leg pads and all the hours of training at last earned me a job in the NHL. I never dreamed that a cup would be named after me when Rune Lantto and the other coaches worked us for countless hours on the ice. (right)

8. Some family visiting us in Toronto. From the left: Agneta Larsson (a childhood friend of Margitta's), my stepfather, Isak, holding Anders, my younger sister Carina, Teresa and me, Margitta, and my mother, Karin. (above)

9. The apples of my eye, Anders and Teresa. (left)

10. Fishing is a relaxing hobby, both in Toronto and in Torne Lake. In this photo, we (Darryl Sittler, his friend, George Ferguson, and I) have caught 17 salmons during two hours of fishing on Lake Ontario. (top)

11. A thousand games with the Maple Leafs meant a party and surprises from the club. They had secretly invited my family and Inge Hammarström to the celebrations. Talk about being surprised! (bottom)

2. NHL official Scotty
   Morrison along
   with teammates
   Greg Terrion and
   Tom Fergus
   present me with
   a silver plate to
   commemorate my
   1,000 games with
   the Maple Leafs.
   (above)

3. What can I say
   about Harold Ballard,
   the Maple Leafs'
   controversial owner?
   In a way, he was like
   a big kid. He was
   always fair to me
   and I think that most
   of the other players
   liked him.
   (above right)

4. Heading up the ice,
   shouting to my
   teammates to pass
   the puck.(right)

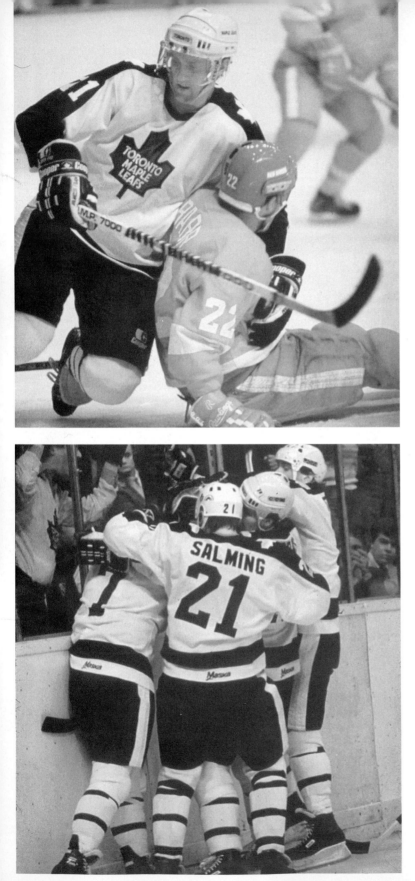

15. Faking out Detro~~
Dave Barrett at t~
blueline.

16. A Leaf celebratio~
along the board~
after an overtime~
goal at the Gard~

The series opened in Philadelphia. We won the first game, 3-2, and came back the second night to win, 4-1. We returned home to the Gardens full of confidence. We took a 3-2 lead into the final minute of Game 3. The Flyers pulled their goalie, Wayne Stephenson, and swarmed our goal. With 38 seconds left, Rick MacLeish scored to send the game into overtime. Four minutes into overtime, MacLeish scored again to give the Flyers a 4-3 victory.

The excitement about this series in Toronto was amazing. The press followed our every move; we could hardly go to the bathroom in peace. Personally, these were fantastically happy days. Our team had friendship, unselfishness, and a determination to work together to win, the essence of team sport. In Philadelphia, they waged an almost psychological war by hiring Kate Smith to sing "God Bless America" before the first game. Her rendition in the packed Spectrum was so powerful and moving that my whole body trembled. But the fourth game was at our home rink. We led 5-2 with six minutes left. Then Kelly let his concentration lapse and we heard him say, "We've got them!"

And then the roof caved in.

Flyer defenceman Tom Bladon made it 5-3. Centre Mel Bridgman, my old nemesis, made it 5-4. When team captain and dogged competitor Bobby Clarke scored next, he sent the game into overtime. The Flyers then scored their fourth consecutive goal for a 6-5 victory, tying the series 2-2.

Leaving the ice, I was crazy with rage. I hate to lose any time, but to lose a three-goal cushion in six minutes was infuriating. As the team trudged into the dressing room, something inside me snapped.

I screamed at Kelly, "Why the hell did you say that!

"How could you say, 'We've got them,' when there was

still time left? You're the coach. It's your job to get us to play hard until the game is over."

He disappeared into his room without a word.

A few minutes later, I felt terrible. I'd never behaved so badly towards a coach. I was ashamed. I knew that it wasn't Red who lost the game. It was us. To this day I don't understand how it happened, but that 6-5 loss finished us. We lost the next two games, 2-0 and 4-3.

After I showered and changed, I went to Red's office. He sat bent over his desk.

"I'm sorry, Red."

I stretched out my hand. He shook it.

"It's okay, Börje."

He was always a classy man. He gave my son Anders his first pair of skates one Christmas. He was also a coach who never lacked an encouraging word when a player was struggling, and who had special ways of motivating us during the playoffs.

It was Kelly who introduced pyramid power to Toronto.

We arrived at the Gardens for a playoff game against the Flyers to find a large pyramid constructed of iron bars in the middle of the dressing room. Red explained how it worked.

"You place yourself in the middle of the pyramid so that all the energy in your body is centralized," he said. "It helps you achieve your maximum strength."

The coach has gone crazy, we joked. We just shook our heads. Pyramid power, indeed.

But athletes are a superstitious group. I know I am. I always put my left shin pad on first, and I like to be the last to leave the dressing room. I remember Dave Keon always used a stick with a straight blade, and after every period he taped it, whether it needed it or not. No one had heard of pyramid power. But, then again, what harm could it do to try it? So before the game everyone took a turn in Red's pyramid. We sat there and hoped to be energized or strengthened or something. To protect against the pyramid's charms wearing off in mid-period, Kelly put several miniature pyramids beneath the players' bench.

If nothing else, Red's pyramids got us thinking about something other than how nervous we all felt. They didn't hurt, but they didn't help a great deal either.

Pyramid power was all well and good, but what we really needed to strengthen our drive to the Stanley Cup were another two or three talented players. We'd done about as well as we could with the team we had. It was a good team, but a notch below the top clubs in the league.

We hoped our fortunes would improve in 1977, when Kelly was replaced by a new coach, Roger Neilson.

Neilson was young and untried, but he gave us a big boost. He was relatively unknown when he was hired from the Peterborough Petes of the Ontario junior league. No legendary former player like so many NHL coaches, Neilson brought competence to the job, rather than old newspaper clippings. He had his own ideas and dared to experiment. He made our practices varied and fun. During games, Neilson was always thinking. He was like a chess master, moving his pieces around, amazing the opposition and even surprising his own team.

On one occasion, he replaced the goalie with an extra skater during the second period. Trailing by several goals, we had a five to three man advantage. It became six to three when our goalie was benched, greatly improving our chances of scoring the goal we needed to get back into the game.

Neilson introduced the NHL to several other innovative manoeuvers. Actually, I always felt he handled his team as

89

though he had a little Swedish blood in him. We liked him because he didn't stand around and scream at us, or run the same practices day in and day out, as most coaches did. NHL coaching generally lacked imagination. Practices would consist of some shooting drills, starts and stops, and other repetitive drills that quickly became boring.

Roger didn't work that way. He discussed theory with us and urged us to contribute ideas. He got close to us while still managing to keep his distance. The knowledgeable hockey fans of Toronto also liked Roger. He is the only coach I've ever seen receive a standing ovation.

Under Neilson, the Leafs became a winning team again, a team capable of competing with the best in the league. We improved our record by 11 points in Neilson's first year, placing sixth overall in the NHL with 92 points. With each victory that season, we could almost feel the temperature rise in Toronto. After two years of losing to Philadelphia in the quarter-finals, we believed we could go further under Neilson's direction.

Our quarter-final opponent was the New York Islanders.

We were the underdogs. The Islanders, building a team that would win four Stanley Cups in the early '80s, had finished the season with 111 points. The series opened on Long Island and we lost both games, 4-3 and 3-2. But we weren't discouraged. We'd played them even and our goalie, Mike Palmateer, was superb. We believed we could win twice in our building.

Incidentally, Palmateer was a terrific goalie. He exuded confidence and played a flamboyant, emotional style. Sometimes, even as the play continued, we could hear him hollering.

"What a save! Did you see that! Whaaat a saaave!"

When the next shot came, he'd be there again to bail us out.

"No sweat, man. I've got it."

What a wonderful guy, and steady as a rock during the playoffs, when motivation and willpower are often as important as ability. Palmateer was just what our team needed to upset a skillful bunch like the Islanders. He was outstanding in Game 3, a 2-0 victory. He followed that with a 3-1 win, and suddenly the series was tied.

But I wouldn't be going back to Long Island.

Midway through Game 3, I left the Gardens in a wheelchair, my eyes bandaged, after Lorne Henning accidentally clipped my right eye with the blade of his stick. I grumbled at the time about having to miss the rest of the playoffs. Looking back, however, I realize how lucky I was not to lose the eye. Without me, the Leafs battled even harder and extended the series to seven games. Palmateer, Sittler, Turnbull, and McDonald were all superb. The seventh game went into overtime, with McDonald scoring in the first extra period to send us into the semi-finals against the Canadiens.

But the Canadiens, in the middle of winning four consecutive Stanley Cups, were too much for us. They easily won the series, 4-0.

This season, 1977-78, was the closest I came to the Stanley Cup. I would have some international success, and play in several all-star games, but, though satisfying, they couldn't erase the disappointment of never bringing a winner to Toronto. There is no feeling like winning a championship with a team that has played hard together for a full season. I'm often asked how it feels to have played so long without once winning the Stanley Cup. Don't I regret it?

The answer is yes, of course I do. Everyone wants to win. But it's not the end of the world. Sport is less important to me now. But, still, it goes without saying that I would have enjoyed at least one chance to drink champagne from the trophy.

I usually watch the Cup finals on TV. My favorite part is when the cameras go into the winning dressing room to record the joyful faces of victory. I can tell how happy the players feel by looking in their eyes. They all have a look of ecstasy and satisfaction that, perhaps, can only be fully appreciated by someone who has experienced a team victory.

I remember when the Calgary Flames won the Cup in 1989. The cameras zoomed in on Lanny McDonald and his eyes had that look. It was wonderful to see him so happy. He deserved it.

10

In the Limelight

===

"Mr. Salming, we've placed a guard at your door so you can be left alone."

The doctor was very friendly.

I was in hospital after being struck in the eye by the stick of New York Islanders' forward Lorne Henning. Because we were in the midst of the playoffs, interest around Toronto in my condition was intense. One vulture from the media even donned a white smock to try to get a bedside interview. The telephone never stopped ringing and I got thousands of letters.

In Sweden, I had heard that Canadians were fanatically interested in hockey. Nevertheless, I was amazed to see how carried away people could become by a game. It was nothing like I'd imagined in my Gävle days. To be part of the adoration that is showered on a Canadian hockey team—or to actually be the centre of attention—was a shock. I never got used to it.

Hockey excites Canadians. They follow their heroes closely in the media. Grown men collect bubble-gum cards of their favorite players, and no one raises an eyebrow. Hockey gossip is part of everyday life. The games are sold out and millions more watch on television.

We find it difficult in Sweden to understand why Canadians remain loyal to a club when players come and go like ordinary employees in any company. But the system is so fundamentally different, and so established, that Canadians would never understand why Swedes don't understand. It all seems natural to them.

There are hundreds of school, junior, and amateur teams in Canada. The best young players' goal is to one day play in the NHL. Everyone loves a competitor whose hard work is eventually rewarded with a career in the NHL. All that the home fans want is for their club to find honest, hard-working players who will help the team win. No one cares if that player comes from Canada, Sweden, or the Soviet Union. As long as he can play, he is accepted, although the fans might root a little bit harder for a hometown boy. But an honest competitor is always loved. And if the club trades such a player, the result can be near-riots in the stands.

In 1979, the Maple Leafs hired a general manager, Punch Imlach, who spent most of his time engaged in personal power plays to better his own position, even at the expense of the team. He traded away the heart of our team, replacing many stars with clearly inferior players.

One of the stars he traded was my friend Lanny McDonald. A skillful right winger with a great shot, McDonald was adored in Toronto. News of his trade enraged Toronto's rabid fans. The Gardens was filled with hand-drawn signs and chants in support of McDonald. On the streets outside, fans organized demonstrations and waved placards.

The fans also protested when Jim Gregory traded Inge to St. Louis in 1977. Inge received dozens of encouraging letters from supporters who would have preferred to see club management traded. The trade seemed so cruel. One day Inge was with us and the next night he was playing for St. Louis. We hardly had time to say goodbye, just a quick, "So long, we'll keep in touch."

But that is the reality of a trade—getting to the next town in time for the next game. Clearing out your apartment, saying goodbye to friends, packing and moving are secondary. They wait until the end of the season.

When McDonald was traded, his wife was two weeks away from giving birth. He commuted between Toronto and Denver for the second half of the season, a trip that could take 10 hours, including time spent waiting for connections.

Hockey can awaken strong emotions in Canadians. Interest in Montreal and Toronto is particularly frenzied. The Canadiens have won 22 Stanley Cup titles, the Maple Leafs 13. They are the two most successful clubs in NHL history.

In cities such as Washington, Buffalo, or St. Louis, the fans would celebrate a Stanley Cup victory and the papers would cover it closely. But if Toronto should win, a carnival atmosphere would envelop the entire city. With only a few exceptions, Maple Leaf Gardens has been sold out for every game since 1947. Its current seating capacity is 16,182. But this number represents only a small fraction of the total number of people who follow the game on radio and television.

Toronto's three newspapers, as well as the radio and TV stations, assign staff to do nothing but report on hockey.

They'll do anything to get a story. When the Leafs are playing well, 10 or 15 reporters could attend a normal practice.

When I arrived, I was unprepared for the fuss that awaited me. It was flattering to be liked, but I would have preferred to be able to stroll down the street or go into a cafe for a sandwich and a beer without dozens of people approaching for autographs or to chat. A hockey player in Toronto never stops working. He is forever being recognized and is expected to be gracious. It took a while before I learned to handle the attention. In the beginning, I just went home, but in time I became resigned to the extra attention that goes with playing for the Maple Leafs.

Toronto fans seemed to respect the fact that I am a private person. Most would shake my hand, say a few words, recognize that I am uncomfortable making small talk with total strangers, then shrug their shoulders and go on their way.

But after a few years, I started to appreciate the fans' appreciation. Canadians are usually relaxed. They are normally polite and well-meaning. The attention became easier for me as I came to understand them better.

But in the mid-seventies, when the Leafs seemed to be putting together a team that could contend for the Stanley Cup, the atmosphere in Toronto was almost hysterical.

The electric hockey climate was tough to handle for a quiet guy from Norrland. But I had to learn. I always signed as many autographs as I could; I remember what it was like to hang around outside the rink and dream of playing with the big guys. It felt right to accommodate children, and even their dads, who usually stammered shyly, "It's for my kid."

I remember seeing Bobby Hull stand and sign autographs for what seemed like hours. If he could find time, then so could I.

Still, when several hundred people are waving auto-graph books, and I am writing and writing and writing and writing, I start to feel like a robot programmed to make people smile by signing my name. It often tried my patience, but during the seventies it was hardest on Anders and Teresa. It couldn't have been fun to go to town with Daddy, and suddenly have him disappear in a sea of people to sign autographs for half an hour.

When I was sick or injured, I received hundreds of get-well letters. I realized that people really do care and at times I was touched by their support.

Here is an example:

Dear Börje,

I saw the picture of you in the Toronto Star where a doc-tor was examining your throat and sinuses, so I thought I would write with some advice which might help you.

I have had a lot of trouble with my sinuses all my life, but just this year I've found a very easy way to ease the problem. I discovered that I was allergic to paper hand-kerchiefs, so I changed to cloth. My sinuses are still not good, but the frequent and irritating attacks have stopped. I hope you try this easy remedy, and I really hope that your health improves so that you can keep your role as the NHL's best defenceman. I have never stopped being surprised and delighted by your great play. If only the Maple Leafs could send the "Big I" [Imlach] and old Harold to the farm club, the club's problems would end quickly instead of blaming them on your ill health.

A faithful, appreciative fan,
Rev. Henry F.M.

Or this one:

Hello Börje!

I have happily followed your hockey success and wish you continued good luck in that tough world. I have also read some of the reports about the illness you are suffering from. I too have suffered from sinusitis for many, many years and have undergone a number of operations and other treatments to try to get rid of the illness.

When everything seemed hopeless I was referred to Huddinge Hospital's ear, nose, and throat clinic and saw Professor Drettner. He is one of Europe's leading authorities in this area, and had just developed a completely new kind of operation. I became the first in Sweden to undergo the treatment. That was four years ago and since then I have been more or less pain free—a wonderful feeling.

The knowledge of the dreadful suffering this illness causes has made me want to share my experiences with you, along with that which finally helped me.

In conclusion, I would like to wish you continued success and better health.

With good wishes,
A. Asta, MÄRSTA

Or this one:

Hello!

You don't know me and I don't know you, other than through unforgettable moments in front of the TV. But because I have had the same problem as you, I thought I would write a few lines and explain how I solved my suffering.

I am a 44-year-old fighter pilot. About 7 years ago, my sinuses started to give me trouble. I don't know why. Perhaps it was because I flew with light colds, and bacteria was pressed into my sinuses by the difference in pressure. Maybe it was because I sweated so much in the cabin, but then, after a hard mission, would take off my helmet on the ground in temperatures of sometimes more than -30 degrees.

But what I am sure of is that neither operations nor long treatments with penicillin or other antibiotics could cure me. There was talk that I shouldn't continue to fly! Anyway, 2 years ago, I started to take an amazing natural medicine that has been known for thousands of years as a cure for this problem. Real Korean GINSENG!

I take a capsule every day and have never felt so well in my life. After three weeks, my sinus problem disappeared completely and has never returned.

I hope you can get rid of your sinusitis, too. I also hope that all goes well for you and Sweden in the Canada Cup.

Keep well and many regards,
Captain B.S. SÅTENÄS

I read all my letters. In the beginning, I tried to answer them personally, but at one point I was receiving several thousand a month. So a couple of other players and I hired a secretary to help us with the replies.

It's a marvellous feeling to be liked and respected for the job you do. Even so, throughout my first three seasons, I underestimated how the Canadians, especially the Toronto fans, felt about me. I always saw myself as a sort of foreign legionnaire who was accepted because I did my job. But I wondered if the affection went any deeper.

The answer came when I represented Sweden in the 1976 Canada Cup. For the first time I was going to play for the opposition in a game at Maple Leaf Gardens. Sweden played Canada in the third game and I wondered how the fans would react to me. Would I be regarded as a traitor, the Maple Leaf defenceman who had come back to sabotage the most important and beloved sports team in Canada? I was very tense before we took the ice.

The first player announced was goalie Hardy Åström. He skated onto the ice and was met by boos.

Then the announcer called, "Börje Salming."

The cheering rose and I felt relief as I glided onto the ice; I hadn't been booed. The crowd had been just as polite earlier in the tournament when Sweden played the USA. But I wasn't surprised to receive applause playing against the Yanks. Hockey emotions between Canada and the USA are similar to the intense feelings between Sweden and Finland.

But I was unsure of what to expect when I skated out to face Canada. The most I'd hoped for was polite applause. And that's how it started. Then something strange, wonderfully strange, started to happen.

The fans all rose from their chairs and started stomping and clapping and cheering like mad. I stood on the blueline waiting for the next name to be announced, but the crowd wouldn't stop. The applause was deafening. I was almost in shock.

"No, this isn't right. It's too much," I thought to myself.

But the crowd continued to cheer. I trembled all over. A couple of minutes passed and I was really feeling awkward. I was embarrassed and didn't know where to go.

"Stop!" I said to myself. "Now, please, you must stop."

If there had been a button to open a trapdoor in the ice, I would have pressed it.

Imagine standing there, just standing there, and being able to do nothing. If I had scored a goal or something, I too could have celebrated. But the game hadn't even started. I skated a few clumsy strides, but the crowd only screamed louder.

It was confusing, impossible to describe. I was moved and near tears. I wouldn't have missed that experience for all the money in the world, but at the same time I wouldn't like to go through it again. A five-minute standing ovation is at least four minutes too long for a boy from Kiruna.

Twelve years later, I had a similar experience before playing my 1,000th game for the Maple Leafs.

"Something's gonna happen today, Börje," said Ballard, tipping me off to a pre-game ceremony.

So at least I had some warning. We gathered at centre ice and out came a Chevrolet Blazer, a gift from the club. But when it pulled up in front of me, out stepped my mother. My heart nearly stopped.

"Congratulations, Börje," she said in her unpretentious way.

Talk about surprises. Ballard had flown her in from Sweden. We embraced in the middle of the ice and the crowd went wild. I was stunned.

"But, Mother, how am I going to be able to play after this?" I whispered in her ear.

It was a fantastic present and a wonderful gesture by the club. The Maple Leafs had brought over my entire family and had also invited Inge Hammarström. I don't remember who won the game that night, and it doesn't really matter. It was a great day in my hockey life.

The only damper on the evening was the sad realization that many other players who had contributed so much to the Maple Leafs never received recognition. Dave Keon and Darryl Sittler, in particular, deserved to have their special nights.

11

No, Thank You, to the President

NHL players are often more like travelling sales reps than professional athletes. They travel constantly. Börje, for instance, travelled about 125,000 Swedish miles during his NHL career.

On average, he played 36 road games a year, travelling an average distance of 106 miles. In addition, there were exhibition games, all-star games, and international games.

The flying distance in kilometres from Toronto to the other NHL cities looks like this:

Los Angeles–3400   Vancouver–3300   Edmonton–2700
Calgary–2250   Winnipeg–1500   Minnesota–1090
St. Louis–1060   Chicago–730   Quebec–720
Boston–670   Washington–640   Philadelphia–620
New York–620   Newark–570   Hartford–520
Montreal–510   Pittsburgh–390   Detroit–330
Buffalo–220

At times in my career, I felt overwhelmed by the demands and pressures of playing in the NHL. On those occasions, I just wanted to escape the hockey scene when I could, even if it meant passing up a trip to the annual NHL all-star game. It was an honor to be chosen for the all-star team and flattering to be wanted, but I reached a point in my career when it became too much.

As the eighties dawned, I decided to apply the brakes. Margitta and I were beginning to drift apart. At the end of each season, my time was divided between charitable functions and my family. For the first few years, it was fun to be involved in various activities, but at the same time it was unfair to Margitta and the children.

So many outside influences strained and tore at our relationship. Maybe it was a fairly normal crisis that all relationships go through sooner or later. I don't know. We suffered for a long time, but in the end I decided to cut down on all engagements outside hockey. We needed time together as a family.

I even declined a dinner invitation to the White House. Out of eight all-star games and dinners, I attended four. Sure, it would have been exciting to meet Ronald Reagan, but I was never comfortable with all the fuss associated with dinners and all-star games. And it didn't seem right to spend more time away from my family.

During breaks and after the season, I wanted to refresh both my body and soul with Margitta and the children.

All-star games are held mostly for show. There is no better example than in 1979, when the NHL used the all-star break to play the Soviet national team in a three-game series called the Challenge Cup. It was the best of the NHL against a hand-picked and thoroughly trained Soviet squad. We had two days to prepare our team; the Soviets had months.

We won the first game, but, unsurprisingly, lost the last two. The score in the deciding game was an embarrassing 6-0.

In the future, maybe I will miss the days when I was so much in demand. It's flattering when so many reporters want to interview me and are interested in what I do and say. That interest is bound to wane as younger, brighter stars inherit the spotlight.

But we'll see what happens in the future. Hockey has given me the financial security to sit back and think about what I want to do with the rest of my life. I can be selective about the projects I choose, and I can decline engagements without feeling that I have let someone down. That freedom feels very good.

I am thankful to Björn Wagnsson and, most of all, to my Toronto lawyer Stephen Duggan, who has helped me with taxes, insurance, and all the details of my contract and financial planning. Stephen has become one of my best friends, and has protected me from a few bad business deals. For example, it became popular a few years ago for players to incorporate as a company to lessen their tax burden. The player would deposit his income in the company and withdraw a salary, thereby decreasing his tax rate by up to 25%. Stephen, however, advised me not to get involved in this scheme.

"I don't think it will work in the long run," he said. "Wait and see."

I followed his advice and did nothing for a year. We were waiting to see if the tax department would clamp down on this practice, but nothing happened.

"What do you think? Maybe I should start my own company," I asked again.

"Wait another year," Stephen replied. "If the authorities don't act next year, then we can assume they have decided to allow this."

Stephen's advice was sound.

The authorities disallowed this obvious tax dodge and pursued several players for back taxes. They had to come up with large lump sum payments.

Professional hockey is just as much show business as sport. We're paid to entertain people who love hockey and excitement. We're also paid to perform so that the team owner can turn a profit and allow the business to continue.

We can't complain; we're well-paid. But the work is demanding and the season long. Teams that advance to the Stanley Cup final can expect to play up to 115 games in a season: about 10 in the pre-season, 80 during the regular schedule, and approximately 25 in the playoffs. The pressure to win is never-ending, and there is little time to relax and relieve the tension.

In a busy week, a team can play five games in eight days, many of them on the road. The competition and the travel can quickly wear you down. If the team is losing, it is easy to become consumed by doubts and depression. The coach is liable to be barking, the newspapers are criticizing, and teammates may be snapping at each other. Inevitably, team spirit sinks and the overall situation worsens.

This scenario unfolded frequently during the eighties, when squabble after squabble disrupted the Maple Leafs. If I had worried too much about all the fighting, I would have gone mad. Instead, I retreated to my home and let my family and friends turn my thoughts to more pleasant matters.

A normal work week is difficult to describe, because there were no normal weeks. Sometimes we'd have only two games, other times four or five. But, to give an example, the itinerary for a two-week period could look like this:

Monday: 11:00 Practice. 13:00 Lunch with the team (voluntary).

Tuesday: 11:00 Practice. 13:00 Lunch with the team. 13:30 Theory before the game (about an hour). 23:00 Curfew.

Wednesday: 10:30 Practice. 12:00 Lunch with the team. 13:00-17:00 Individual relaxation, sleep. 18:00 Meeting and warm-up. 20:00 Game against the Washington Capitals.

Thursday: 11:00 Practice. 13:00 Lunch with the team (voluntary).

Friday: 11:00 Practice. 18:30 Meeting at the airport, travel. 20:00 Arrival in Detroit, bus to hotel. 23:00 Curfew.

Saturday: 08:30 Wake, breakfast. 10:00 Bus to Joe Louis Arena. 11:30 Practice. 13:30 Lunch at the hotel, theory. 15:00-17:00 Relaxation, sleep. 17:00 Bus to Joe Louis Arena. 19:30 Game against the Red Wings. 22:15 Bus to the airport. 23:00 Flight to Toronto. 00:45 Home.

Sunday: 11:00 Practice.

Monday: 10:30 Practice. 12:00 Lunch with the team. 13:00 Bus to Buffalo. 17:00 Warm-up, Memorial Auditorium. 19:30 Game against the Buffalo Sabres. 22:15 Bus to Toronto. 01:30 Home.

Tuesday: 11:00 Practice, theory. 13:00 Lunch with the team (voluntary). 23:00 Curfew.

Wednesday: 10:30 Practice. 12:00 Lunch with the team. 14:00-17:00 Individual relaxation, sleep. 18:00 Meeting and warm-up. 20:00 Game against the Vancouver Canucks. 22:45 Bus to the airport. 00:15 Flight to New York. 01:15 Arrival in New York, bus to hotel.

Thursday: 09:00 Wake, breakfast. 10:00 Bus to practice arena. 11:00 Practice. 13:30 Lunch at the hotel, theory. 15:00-17:00 Relaxation, sleep. 17:00 Bus to Madison Square Garden. 19:30 Game against the Rangers. 22:15 Bus to airport. 00:00 Flight to Toronto. 02:00 Home.

Friday: 11:30 Practice. 13:00 Lunch with the team (voluntary).

Saturday: 10:30 Practice. 11:30 Lunch with the team. 12:15 Bus to the airport, theory. 13:30 Flight to Quebec. 14:30 Arrival, bus to Colisée. 17:30 Meeting and warm-up. 19:30 Game against the Nordiques. 22:15 Bus to the airport. 23:30 Flight to Toronto. 02:00 Home.

Sunday: 11:00 Practice.

Whew!

It's tough to believe I actually carried on like that for 17 years. But I'm not complaining. When I was busy running between my home, the rink, and the airport, the time went fast. Of course it was tiring, but anyone who has played team sports knows the rewards of practising hard together and striving for a common goal in competition. Still, it sometimes got tedious. It was like being stuck on a treadmill: bus, airport, hotel, breakfast, practice, lunch, nap, strategy, and game. Then you'd do it all again the next day.

Anyone who travels frequently knows that hundreds of hours are lost waiting for buses, taxis, hotel keys, luggage, airline tickets, etc. What makes hockey players different is that we must endure this tedious routine several times a week. We're always waiting—a teammate who overslept, a table at a restaurant, a caretaker to unlock the dressing room. An impatient person would go nuts in a single season if he let all the waiting get to him. Luckily, however, it isn't the players' job to organize all the travel details.

I usually passed the time by reading (mostly detective and adventure novels) or sleeping.

Understandably, the boredom of travel led to an occasional display of rowdy behavior as players released pent-up tension. Nothing scandalous, mind you. We'd go out for a good meal, have a couple of beers, and, of course, admire pretty girls. Occasionally, someone would lose control and say something stupid, or lose a room key, or get involved in the type of foolishness that can happen when 20 guys get together.

But, on the whole, it was innocent fun.

One time in Chicago during the seventies, we were snowed in and the game was cancelled. I was injured but was with the team on crutches. The Black Hawks invited us to dinner, along with the bus driver. It turned into a long night and the driver found it difficult to take us back to the hotel. The roads were deep with snow and slush. He crawled along as best he could, but got stuck a short distance from the hotel.

We all filed off the bus and within seconds were involved in the biggest snowball fight ever to hit Chicago. Snowballs flew all around the bus. Even Red Kelly got hit in the head. I tossed away my crutches and joined in as best I could, which didn't impress the coaches. That was the last time injured players were allowed to accompany the team on the road. It was great fun, but our biggest laugh came the next morning.

"Look!" yelled one of the guys, laughing and pointing out the hotel window.

The snow plough had been by. The road was clear, but our bus was nowhere near the road. It was still stranded on a boulevard, covered in snow with the doors left wide open.

12

Canada Cup

Expectations were high throughout the hockey world before the 1976 Canada Cup. After years of waiting, all the best players in the world were finally to be gathered together for one tournament. There was no debate about professionals or amateurs; the competition was open to the best players from each nation. Period.

The event was organized by Alan Eagleson, a lawyer and player agent, who overcame several obstacles to bring this dream tournament to fruition. Owners of NHL and WHA clubs were reluctant to release their best players because of the risk of injury. In Europe, there were other kinds of doubts. Club owners in Scandanavia feared that their best players would be noticed by their NHL and WHA rivals and disappear from Swedish and Finnish hockey. The Soviets and Czechs worried about defections.

When agreement to play the tournament was finally reached, many experts predicted a slaughter by the American *and Canadian ruffians. The slaughter, however, never happened.*

As far as Börje was concerned, the tournament showed all of Sweden how big a star he had become in Toronto and in the NHL. His five-minute ovation at Maple Leaf Gardens was astounding. Then, when he scored twice in Sweden's 2-1 victory over Czechoslovakia at the Quebec Colisée, the Gardens' scoreboard lit up: Salming 2, Czechoslovakia 1.

Swedish players welcomed the Canada Cup with open arms. For a Swedish amateur, the world championships had for years represented the pinnacle of his career. The Canada Cup, by bringing together the best talent in the world, took these players one step higher. They recognized, however, that the competition wouldn't be easy.

The Soviets were as professional as any team in the world, maybe even more so than the NHL professionals. All their best players were on the same club, Moscow's Red Army team. Their teamwork was exquisite and they pretty much won at will against the semi-professional Czechs and the largely amateur Swedes and Finns.

Canada's professionals also looked forward to the Canada Cup. Some people say that Canadian professionals only play for money, that they have no allegiance to their national team. But these people are wrong. Canadians are extremely patriotic and consider it an honor to wear the red maple leaf jersey. History has shown that intense international competition brings out the best in their game.

NHL professionals are used to playing a long schedule to determine who will make the playoffs. They know that the key to playoff success lies less in skating and playmaking than in learning to cope with the extreme pressure. Players must be able to stay calm, concentrate on the task at hand,

and not get caught up in the hysteria. These qualities serve Canadians well in tournaments like the Canada Cup.

The Swedish team gathered in Gothenburg in August. We were anxious to begin the first tournament in which professionals would represent Tre Kronor. Our team looked strong. We had Juha Widing, who walked around in his slippers with a towel wrapped around his summer girth. The extra weight gave him the look of a seasoned NHL professional. Then there was the gang from Winnipeg: Thommie Bergman, Willy Lindström, Ulf "Lill-Pröjsan" Nilsson, Anders Hedberg, Dan Labraaten, and Lars-Erik Sjöberg or "Dachshund", a short man but a leader nonetheless.

We had 10 professionals among the 25 players chosen by coach "Virus" Lindberg. Unsurprisingly, before camp started, we had a squabble with the Swedish Hockey Federation. We wanted insurance to protect us in case of injury. Our coverage by the NHL and WHA didn't apply when we played for the national team. The Canada Cup was breaking new ground in international hockey and, as a result, there was considerable confusion. The Federation hadn't even considered insurance, and when they balked at providing coverage we threatened to walk out.

It was unfortunate that the situation had to come to this. We were accused of playing only for money, but that criticism was unfair. Hockey was our livelihood. In North America, we all had extensive coverage to protect us in the event of a career-ending injury. It would have been foolish for us to put not only our careers but our financial future at risk by playing without proper insurance.

It turned out that three Winnipeg players were injured (Willy Lindström, Thommie Bergman, and Dan Labraaten), so it was fortunate that we had fought for proper insurance.

It's possible that the Federation was still angry at us for moving to North America. Perhaps they were irritated that we had accepted the challenge of a lifetime when the best league in the world courted us with promises of wealth and adventure. Then again, maybe the Federation genuinely didn't understand our situation.

They had been nonchalant in their dealings with us from the day the Canada Cup was announced. Instead of a letter enquiring about our availability or even asking if we were interested, we received a terse notice that read, "Negotiate with your club about playing for Sweden in the Canada Cup."

This was an ill-advised way to go about business. It wasn't our job to negotiate with our individual employers. Gaining our release was a task for the Federation, working in conjunction with agents and lawyers who could draft an agreement acceptable to all parties. The players were hardly in a position to stroll into the club owners' offices and announce: "It looks like Sweden wants me to play for the national team. I'll see you later."

We players felt caught in the middle. We understood that the owners had legitimate concerns, primarily regarding injuries. They'd invested heavily in us and we felt an obligation to support the club and the league as best we could. But we were also eager to represent our country. What we needed was a third party to intercede with the owners on our behalf. None of us wanted a direct showdown with our bosses because, even if we won, we would still have to play for them after the Canada Cup.

The atmosphere on the team and with the team managers was never a problem. "Virus" found the right recipe to get us to play together. He easily shifted from being one of the gang, casually tapping our NHL experience to help formulate strategy, to stepping back and making it clear that the final decisions were his. He was yet another example of a good Swedish coach.

We opened the tournament at Maple Leaf Gardens against the US. The Americans got ugly right at the beginning, and before the game was six minutes old, they'd collected 25 minutes in penalties. But their intimidation tactics didn't work. We led 5-0 after the first period and coasted to a 5-2 victory.

The next evening, I took the team to my favorite restaurant, Hy's. Their steaks are unbelievable, big and juicy. I worried that a few of the guys, those who hadn't been to Canada before, would eat until they exploded. Göran Högosta and Wille Löfqvist, the backup goalies who mostly watched from the bench because Hardy Åström was so masterful, did, in fact, gain several pounds during the competition. So did Lars-Göran Nilsson, who also seldom played. Aside from the odd case of heartburn, the evening at Hy's was a success, an ideal way to break the tension before our tough test two days later.

The Soviets, looking weaker than usual, had opened the tournament with a 5-3 loss to Czechoslovakia. We knew their mood would be ornery when they faced us. But again our power play was clicking and we took a 2-0 lead. But the Soviets never wavered from their methodical tap-tap-tap style, while we drew back into a defensive posture that seldom works against a strong offensive team like the Soviets.

When Kapustin put the Soviets ahead, 3-2, in the middle of the last period, many TV viewers must have believed that Sweden was finished. On the ice, however, we knew we had more to give. "Virus" drove me hard and I felt great. It was as if I was back at the 1973 world championships—on one side surrounded by my many friends in blue and yellow, on the other, facing the strong, emotionless Soviets in red.

With a couple of minutes left in the game, I saw a hole open up in the middle of the ice and I broke for it. I reached the puck and nudged it forward to Anders Hedberg who had a breakaway. Hedberg skated in alone on Tretiak and scored to tie the game. What a feeling!

Back home, the press had widely speculated that the Canada Cup would be a trans-Atlantic blood bath for Sweden. They figured that we'd be slaughtered. But the writers overlooked the fact that the best Canadian players have never been brawlers or cheats.

I encountered no unsportsmanlike behaviour, on or off the ice. The Canadians played hard but fair. They targeted Hedberg and me for special attention, never missing an opportunity to take us into the boards. Bobby Hull landed a couple of really hard hits at the beginning of the game, but the hits were clean.

When we played them, Canada got an early goal, a bad omen for us. No team is more difficult to stop than Canada when it has an advantage. They never try to defend their lead, but always continue to attack, to push forward and press their advantage. Still, I thought we played well. We created some good scoring chances but their goalie, Rogatien Vachon, had a great day.

Despite the defeat, Sweden still had a good chance to earn a place in the playoffs. So what happened? Finland, of course.

To this day, I still can't fathom the reasons for our downfall. All I know is that it happened. It wasn't that we underestimated the Finns; we talked before the game about how tough they could play, particularly against their arch rival, Sweden. Before the game, we reminded each other that, for Finland, a victory over Sweden was the next best thing to winning the whole tournament. And it wasn't just Lindberg, our coach, who warned us to be vigilant. Our team had a solid core of North American professionals who were anxious to demonstrate that life abroad had made them better hockey players. The amateurs in our midst were just as keen because they wanted to attract the attention of the pro scouts. So our humiliation was a team effort.

Perhaps the game was too easy in the beginning. Two minutes into the second period, Mats Åhlberg scored to give us a 4-1 lead. Everything was going our way. Then, just as quickly, the tide turned. The final score was 8-5 for Finland. Lasse Oksanen (a professional in Italy) scored the winning and insurance goals.

Maybe it was the depressing atmosphere in Winnipeg that put us off. The stands were almost silent, a far cry from the electricity that filled the air in Montreal and Toronto.

I was ashamed. The professionals had let the team down. Our amateurs did all we asked of them. As it happened, the defeat mattered less after the Czechs beat Canada 1-0. But, still, the Finnish victory was depressing. They had been the tournament punching bag, losing 11-2 to Canada, 8-0 to Czechoslovakia, and 11-3 to the Soviets before they humbled us.

We played only for honor in our final game against Czechoslovakia. The Czechs had already advanced to the final. We had a chance to show that we should also have been there. As well, I'd played poorly against Finland and saw the Czech game as my chance for redemption.

Both goalies, Sweden's Göran Högosta and Czechoslovakia's Dzurilla, played brilliantly. But the Czechs took the lead. In the second period, we had a five to three man advantage for nearly a minute. Lars-Erik Sjöberg and

Ulf Nilsson worked the power play superbly. They moved the puck back and forth between them and then passed it off to me. My shot, hard and accurate, beat Dzurilla and the game was tied.

Our play had washed away the dusty residue of shame left over from the Finnish game. That I was able to decide the match was of some comfort, although nothing could fully erase my anguish at losing to Finland. We should have been in the final; that's still how I feel today.

Canada and Czechoslovakia met in the final, and it was no surprise that Canada won the title with two straight victories. The Canadians are talented, but more than that, they play best when it matters most. To reach the final, Canada had to get by the Soviets in a one-game playoff. The Czechs, winners of the round robin portion of the tournament, were waiting for them. Because Canada had lost 1-0 to the Czechs in the round robin many expected the final to be close. But Canada won the first game 6-0 and it was all over.

True, the Czechs played better in the second game, but Canada was always in control. The game went into overtime tied 4-4 and Darryl Sittler scored the winner.

The first game had been played in Toronto, and Alan Eagleson was keen that I present the award to the player selected as the outstanding performer of the game. Still incredibly shy, I was reluctant.

"Please, get somebody else," I begged Eagleson.

He disappeared without a word, and I thought I was off the hook. Björn Wagnsson was in the stands, and towards the end of the game he dragged me down to ice level.

"You can at least choose the player of the match," Björn suggested, to which I agreed.

I figured that I would tell Eagleson my choice, Bobby Orr, and then I could return to my seat. But Eagleson and Wagnsson had other plans.

When Orr's name was announced, Wagnsson and Eagleson grabbed hold of my arms and all but dragged me onto the red carpet that led to centre ice. Simultaneously, Orr started to come forward. With 16,000 people in the stands and millions more watching on television, I could hardly struggle, or knock down the two lawyers (although I was tempted). My only recourse was to go along and present the prize to Orr, a fine guy and great player.

Today I am grateful to Eagleson and Wagnsson. Congratulating Orr at centre ice of Maple Leaf Gardens is a proud memory for me. Without doubt, the entire 1976 Canada Cup tournament ranks among my greatest hockey experiences. The same, unfortunately, cannot be said of the 1981 Canada Cup.

It was one big disappointment.

The expectations for Team Sweden were much higher by 1981. Our team comprised almost entirely NHL professionals (the WHA had folded in 1979) who were accustomed to playing on the smaller North American rinks. We had only six amateurs: Patrik Sundström, Göte Wälitalo, Pekka Lindmark, Peter Helander, Jan Erixon, and Mats Waltin.

We opened with a 3-1 loss to the USA and followed that game by losing 6-3 to the Soviet Union. Next, we beat Finland, 5-0. We led by only one goal going into the third period, so the game was closer than the score might indicate. It felt good to win a tough game, but the satisfaction was fleeting. We didn't win another game. It was typical that we beat the Finns when it didn't matter after losing to them in 1976 when we absolutely needed a victory. I cannot explain what happened in 1981. We were disgracefully bad. I have almost completely forgotten the tournament.

Just the same, it was fun to be involved in the first two Canada Cups. Besides participating in a terrific competition, I had the chance to become better acquainted with the other Swedish professionals. Many of them had arrived on the scene after I'd left for Canada in 1973. I knew them by reputation but not personally. The hectic schedule in the NHL allows for nothing more than a quick introduction and perhaps a short chat. Then it's off to the bus and the next stop. Being able to socialize away from the rink with my Swedish peers alone made the experience of the Canada Cups worthwhile.

13

Downhill with Punch

The Toronto Maple Leafs' success in 1978, when they upset the New York Islanders to advance to the NHL semifinals, caused the city's hockey thermometer to rise to a feverish level. In Montreal, the arch-rival Canadiens were in the middle of four consecutive championships. The feeling in Toronto was that the Maple Leafs could be the club to break the string. As always when the air heats up with the promise of success, reality can get lost behind a cloud of dreamy expectation. That's what happened in Toronto. Upper management began talking about the grand old days and demanded an instant return to the glory of yesteryear.

Sometime during the 1978-79 season, Leafs' owner Harold Ballard decided that Roger Neilson's coaching methods weren't producing quick enough results. Soon the papers were also writing about Neilson, complaining that his style of hockey was boring and unimaginative.

After our 92-point season of 1977-78, everyone expected us to climb past 100 points in '78-79 and compete with the best teams in the NHL. It was a feeling shared by management, coaches, players, the media, and the fans. But for many reasons we couldn't pull the magic rabbit of success out of the hat. In fact, we regressed and Neilson found himself under fire from Ballard and the press.

The players, however, stood squarely behind Neilson. We never stopped believing in him and trusted that his long-range plan would reap dividends. But NHL hockey is anything but a patient game. Soon rumors began spreading that Neilson was about to be fired. Before a game in Montreal, Neilson himself hinted to us that something was likely to happen. Ballard had apparently told the press that if we lost to the Canadiens, Neilson was finished. For Neilson's sake as well as our own, we dug in and played a great game against the Stanley Cup champions, but lost nevertheless, 2-1.

In the dressing room afterwards, Neilson was calm.

"Thanks, guys. You played a fantastic game.

"Unfortunately, it was my last. I've been fired."

We couldn't believe it.

It made no sense to fire Neilson in mid-season.

This was something new for me. I'd seen players traded and demoted, and knew that coaches sometimes got fired. But in the middle of the season? How stupid could management be?

Team captain Darryl Sittler and several other players set out to save Roger. They had intensive discussions with Ballard and general manager Jim Gregory. Sittler told the boss that we supported Roger and wanted him back. It was Ballard alone who would make the final decision.

As usual, he had been quoted widely in the press about Neilson's firing. Ballard's problem was to find a solution without losing face, either with us or the public. Finally, he found the answer. He'd make a joke out of the entire episode.

Ballard's suggestion was that we would skate onto the ice for our next game without a coach. A few minutes later, just before the opening face-off, Neilson would appear wearing a paper bag over his head. Then, with a dramatic gesture, he'd lift the bag and, to the delight of everyone, reveal that he was still coaching the Leafs.

That was the plan. But Neilson refused to play along. He told Ballard he'd welcome reinstatement to his old job, but he wouldn't play the buffoon. And Ballard finally agreed.

Ballard was like that. It would never have occurred to him that he was hurting a decent man like Roger. He was a showman first and a serious hockey executive second. In his own way, Ballard wanted what was best for the Maple Leafs, but his methods were, to say the least, curious. Beginning with the paper bag fiasco, his management style grew more and more eccentric. In the meantime, while Ballard toyed with Neilson, the players had no idea who was supposed to coach the team. Finally, right before game time, Roger entered the dressing room—without a bag—and informed us, to our relief, that he had been rehired. When Roger appeared behind the bench, the crowd went wild. They gave the coach a standing ovation. Some fans carried signs that expressed their view of the zany happenings. One, for example, read simply: "The hell with Harold."

Excited to have Roger back, we beat the Philadelphia Flyers, 4-3, and we followed that win with four more in succession. It was the best way to express how we felt about our abused coach.

We made the play-offs with 81 points, a drop of 11 from the previous year. Our first-round opponent was the Atlanta Flames and we won the best-of-three mini-series in two games. More memorable than the results, however, was the plane ride to Atlanta. After finishing our regular schedule in Boston, we flew directly to Atlanta. On the way, we encountered a bad storm and fierce turbulence. After landing in Atlanta, we had to spend an hour recuperating at the airport because everyone looked green and felt terrible.

We were fine by the next night, however, and won 2-1 in a brawl-filled game. Five or six guys from each team were ejected. The second game was in Toronto and we won again, advancing to the quarter-finals against the Canadiens. They beat us in four straight.

The relationship between Neilson and management remained ice-cold. The coach, with his innovative coaching style, didn't speak the same hockey language as Ballard. So Neilson was fired.

Ballard yearned for a return to the good old days. He wanted someone who had already experienced the joy of winning the Stanley Cup, someone who had been there before. He didn't understand that a hungry young team with a hungry young coach could also be effective if allowed to work in peace and quiet.

And if firing Neilson wasn't bad enough, the error was compounded when general manager Jim Gregory was also canned. To the players, Gregory's firing signalled that something tragic was about to befall the Maple Leafs. Gregory was admired and respected, a GM who handled the press and players well. He also knew a lot about hockey. But Ballard obviously thought Gregory was too soft. He wanted a tougher hand steering the Leafs.

Ballard's answer was Leonard "Punch" Imlach.

Imlach arrived from Buffalo, where he had been general manager of the Sabres, but he was already famous in Toronto for coaching the Leafs to four Stanley Cup championships in the 1960s, including the Leafs' last Cup in 1967. He became the Leafs' new general manager and head coach, although Floyd Smith and Dick Duff carried out the actual coaching chores. Officially, Smith was the coach and Duff his assistant. But they were nothing but marionettes completely controlled by Imlach.

In his contract with Ballard, Imlach was guaranteed autonomy to run the club as he saw fit. Ballard's penchant for interfering was well-known and Imlach wanted none of it. He insisted on having the final say regarding personnel.

And that was the beginning of the end.

Imlach traded players almost haphazardly, although an unsettling pattern soon emerged. Clever, independent, skillful players were often replaced by older, discarded players whom Imlach knew, players Imlach was confident he could control. Two or three of them had already retired when Imlach offered them contracts. One was Carl Brewer. He had been a great Leaf defenceman during the '60s, but to haul him out of retirement did nothing for team morale.

Lanny McDonald was the team representative to the NHL Players' Association, the players' union, and Imlach didn't like it. He believed the Maple Leafs could have only one boss—Imlach.

"Give that up or I'll trade you," Imlach told McDonald.

When the team heard about the ultimatum, we were all concerned. Imlach was liable to do anything. The atmosphere around the team became strained, our play suffered, and the papers wrote madly about trade rumors. No Stanley Cup could be won in that environment.

It's hard to understand management's thinking.

In the end, opposition to Imlach became so widespread that he wanted to trade both McDonald and Darryl Sittler— a real touch of genius. Two seasons previous, Sittler was third overall in NHL scoring, while McDonald was tenth. They were our two best offensive players, and two of the best in the entire league.

Sittler, who usually told Imlach what he thought, had a no-trade clause in his contract. But that didn't stop Imlach from finding a way to get at Darryl. Imlach's answer was to trade McDonald, Sittler's best friend. It was a spiteful move by Imlach that infuriated the Toronto fans who loved McDonald. Many of them arrived at the next game with hand-painted signs that demanded Imlach's head on a platter.

Darryl was so angry he ripped the captain's "C" from his sweater. He refused to have anything to do with team management after that. He explained his actions in a press release:

"I have tried to carry out my responsibilities as team captain in an honest and proper way. I forwarded the players' viewpoints to the club management and forwarded the club management's views to the players.

"At the beginning of the season I was sued by the club. They said that it wasn't anything personal. I explained my position to Mr. Imlach and Mr. Ballard, that the captain's duty is to work with both players and management, not solely for the management.

"Mr. Ballard and Mr. Imlach made some negative statements about me and my teammates a few weeks ago, and I met them later to discuss these statements. They thought that I was too sensitive.

"Generally I have had little contact with Mr. Imlach, and now it is clear to me that he and I have completely different ideas concerning communication between the players and management.

"I have recently learned that the management has tried to hinder me for taking part in *Hockey Night In Canada* TV broadcasts.

"I spend more and more time with the player/management problems, but I feel that I cannot achieve enough for my teammates. The war between Mr. Eagleson and Mr. Imlach should not overshadow the most important matter—the Toronto Maple Leafs.

"I am completely loyal to the Toronto Maple Leafs. I will not desert my teammates. But I must be honest with myself. I will continue to fight for the players' rights. but not as captain of the team.

"What I want to do now is to direct all my energy and all my power towards my team as a player."

The quarrel between Eagleson and Imlach that Sittler mentioned began because of a hockey skills competition, *Showdown*, in which I also competed. *Showdown* was a skating, passing, and shooting contest between NHL players made exclusively for television. The one summer I participated, I was injured, which angered Leaf management.

When Darryl and Mike Palmateer were invited to take part the following year, Imlach tried to stop them. The players, through the Players' Association executive director Alan Eagleson, refused to back down. There was a lot of arguing and in the end Sittler and Palmateer did indeed participate, despite Imlach's objections. The feud between Imlach and Sittler escalated from there.

Where did I figure in this mess?

I remained quiet in the dressing room, although I was deeply troubled. I felt sorry that such animosity had developed and frightened to think of what it might mean to me and the team. Punch's power struggle had nothing at all to do with hockey. It was a stupid matter of ego. I didn't want to get involved. I wanted to play hockey.

That is how I approached all the controversies that seemed to forever envelop the Maple Leafs. I tried to stay in the background, which sometimes frustrated my teammates.

Darryl said to me many times, "Hell, Börje, you've got to speak up too."

I never did.

I struggled to find something useful to say. I wanted to help Darryl. He was a good guy and a great captain who never stopped working for the team, on and off the ice.

At night, I often lay awake thinking about what I should say. Sometimes I had it all worked out: I will say this and that and then everything will be all right.

Then day would dawn and I would become speechless. I could find neither the right opportunity nor the right words.

I know the difference between right and wrong, but I have never been good at leading others. I've never been a talker. I like to work together with people in a positive way. It's easy to complain and be opinionated, but difficult to find solutions to problems.

I felt I had no solution, nothing better to suggest. What good would it do if I too complained?

So I suffered. In silence.

When Imlach cut out the heart of the team, he bled me of my enthusiasm. I did my job, but I didn't have the same spark. It was obvious that the Maple Leafs were going nowhere. That realization weighed heavily on me. Besides, there was always the possibility that Imlach might also trade me. I knew it could happen but hoped that reason would prevail. We liked Toronto. Anders and Teresa had friends and were comfortable in school. I might have been able to earn more money else-where, but I wanted to stay in Toronto—although I resolved that Imlach would have to work hard to get my signature on a new contract. He treated people like shit.

In the spring of 1980, Imlach offered to extend my con-tract. His proposal, however, was insulting. It included a lot of complicated performance bonuses. I've never liked that type of deal. I prefer a straightforward contract with all the money guaranteed, regardless of injuries, slumps, or other potential complications.

I rejected his offer.

"I'll play out my option year," I said.

"Ha, option year," Imlach scoffed. "You'll end up somewhere with a bad contract."

At the end of the season, I went home as usual. In June, Imlach phoned and said he wanted to come to Stockholm to negotiate.

Björn Wagnsson and I met him at the Sheraton Hotel. As usual, Imlach was cross with me. We had never had a direct argument or any type of personal quarrel. Still, he rarely spoke to me, except to shout at me occasionally after a game. On the other hand, I never spoke to him either. I preferred to act as if he wasn't there.

"I'll give you $250,000 for five years. That's as far as I can go," Imlach said.

He went home without my signature.

There was a lot of talk in Toronto that summer. I was glad to be in Sweden away from it, and glad that Björn was handling the negotiations. Imlach seemed preoccupied with finding a way to get rid of Sittler. Among other discussions, he was believed to have had long, involved talks with the Calgary Flames. According to the rumors, Imlach nearly agreed to send Sittler to Calgary for three players, including Kent Nilsson. Ballard heard of the talks and seemed to like the idea. He began to tell the papers about the good players the Leafs might get.

Imlach was incensed to learn that Ballard had talked to the press about the possible deal. A few days later, Imlach was sent to hospital with a heart attack.

When I reported to training camp, my contract was still unresolved. I had no idea what was going to happen. The New York Rangers and Quebec Nordiques were apparently interested in acquiring me, and I was prepared to move, although I didn't want to. After practice one morning, Ballard came into the dressing room and approached me in the shower. "Börje, I'll give you $300,000," he said.

He extended his hand.

"No, Harold," I replied. "Not in the shower. You know I've got to speak with Björn first."

Björn called Ballard and they agreed on a five-year contract that paid me $350,000 for the first three years and $400,000 for the final two. I was satisfied. For that kind of money, I thought it was worth staying in Toronto, working hard and hoping for better times.

Imlach had another heart attack before the 1981 season. His relationship with Ballard had been souring and Ballard used Imlach's ill health as an excuse to get rid of him. Ballard had gotten the message that the players didn't like Imlach.

We got a new general manager, Gerry McNamara (the same man who had visited me in Brynäs's changing room in 1972), and a new coach, Mike Nykoluk, but the changes came too late to restore all that Imlach had destroyed. Only two guys remained from the team I joined in 1973. Clearly, it was going to take a long time to rebuild.

As one of the few Leaf veterans, there was pressure on me to assume a leadership role on the team.

The new, young players looked up to me, and some of them even admitted that I had been their boyhood idol. Unfortunately, since Imlach's arrival on the scene, an invisible wall had developed between the coaches and me. They seemed to be scared of me.

That barrier was not of my doing. I just played hockey. I did the best I could, but I never said much; I left the talking to others. I had no wish to be some kind of guru who was expected to know everything about the game. I didn't demand that young players think like me or play like me. And I didn't want to interfere with the way the coaches did their job. If I had an opinion about a particular aspect of a game, I expressed it in the dressing room. I never made a big deal about it; I just considered it my small part in helping us win the game. But some coaches interpreted my advice as a challenge to their authority. Or even a threat.

So what was I supposed to do?

Sometimes I anguished a little over refusing to accept the team captaincy. It takes many attributes to be a good captain. The honor shouldn't go to the player who is the most experienced or the most talented. A captain must be able to negotiate with team management and represent the club at all types of functions away from the rink.

I walk away from quarrels if I can, and that is probably why I have landed in a few strange situations—like the time coach John Brophy sent me home after a match in 1987.

We were in a hotel in Minneapolis after a 4-3 defeat to the North Stars. The next morning we were to travel to Detroit for a game the following night. One of the guys had bought a Nerf basketball set, a small basket and a spongy ball, as a present for his son. To kill the time while 10 of us waited for the delivery of a pizza, we started fooling around with the toy.

It was just innocent fun, but it got too noisy. The front desk called the room and told us that guests were complaining. We promised to be quieter, but before long we were as loud as ever. This time, hotel staff called Brophy and threatened to call the police if we didn't calm down. No one told us about the second call.

A short time later, there was a pounding at the door. It was the police. Six guys climbed out the ground-floor window and disappeared. I stayed behind. Someone had to open the door.

"What's going on here?" asked the officer.

Three teammates and I were thrown out of the hotel. We ended up at a neighboring hotel, spending the night in the lobby playing cards. But Brophy held me responsible. The next day, he sent me home and the team played in Detroit with only five defencemen.

Admittedly, we had been noisy. But the hotel staff contacted Brophy so he could put a lid on the mischief before things got out of hand. Had he knocked on our door, or even phoned, the police might never have been called. True, as the oldest player in the group, perhaps I should have forced the guys to stop. It was all just playful fun, though, nothing like the wild goings-on Brophy hinted at to the media.

I think Brophy was looking for a reason to get rid of me. After that incident, Ballard was actually eager to trade me. But the other players stuck up for me, and so did the press. Some reporters declared that the punishment had been absurd.

I felt unfairly treated and refused to practise until the club apologized publicly. It was the first time in my career that I decided to be difficult. But I was determined not to be scapegoated just because I was the best-known player in the group.

In the end, the apology came. Management talked to the hotel staff and realized a minor incident had been blown way out of proportion. The letter of apology was signed by Ballard himself.

14

Ballard
and Me

===

Harold Ballard was one of a kind. From his birth near the beginning of the century to his death in 1990 at the age of 86, he engaged in all manner of mischief and controversy.

His life is detailed in miles of newspaper copy, as well as in three books.

Börje doesn't know why Ballard protected him, but it was probably due to Börje's easygoing personality and his phenomenal capacity to work on the ice.

Off the ice, Börje remained distant from the many controversies that swept Maple Leaf Gardens. He always preferred to avoid confrontation. He played hockey and played it well, which satisfied Ballard, who insisted on making all the decisions while demanding loyalty and results. And loyalty was most important of all.

Ballard was born in 1903 in Paris, a small town not far from Toronto. His father ran his own business manufacturing, among other products, skate blades. Harold liked to describe himself as a successful speed skater, but the archives don't substantiate his claims.

Ballard did, however, drive a speedboat during the 1920s, and had a fair amount of success in races around Toronto.

During the '30s, Ballard was a guy who enjoyed the fun things in life, but he also worked hard in his father's factory. He was frequently seen at big sporting events, especially hockey matches, and was soon involved as an amateur team manager.

In 1927, Conn Smythe bought Toronto's NHL team, the St. Pats, one of the weakest teams in the league. The story goes that a group of American businessmen wanted to move the St. Pats to Philadelphia, but Smythe convinced the St. Pats owners to sell to him. Although his offer was lower, the team would remain in Toronto.

Smythe renamed the team the Maple Leafs, shamelessly borrowing the maple leaf crest from the Canadian Olympic team. As the years passed, the Leafs drew large crowds, and Maple Leaf Gardens, with a seating capacity of 13,500, was built in 1931.

Smythe hired Ballard during the 1940s to work for the junior team, the Toronto Marlboros. He was responsible for ticket sales, team travel, and various other duties. He began to get a reputation for being an able organizer with a flair for public relations. In 1961, Smythe retired and passed the operation of the Maple Leafs to a committee with John W. Bassett as the chairman. The press soon nicknamed the committee the Silver Seven. They were a happy bunch of guys, mostly in their forties, who often travelled with the team, enjoying all the perks of their prestigious position.

Ballard, who was approaching 60, was the most energetic member of the group. He seemed to have an endless appetite for work and for partying.

Eventually, a power struggle ensued with Bassett on one side and Ballard on the other. Ballard won.

In 1971, Bassett sold his shares in Maple Leaf Gardens to Ballard and Stafford Smythe, Conn Smythe's son. After Stafford died later that year, Ballard bought all the shares controlled by Smythe's estate, thereby winning controlling interest in the hockey club. He remained the boss until his death in 1990.

A Toronto sportswriter once described his job of covering Ballard's Leaf teams as follows:

"When I was young, I dreamed of working at a circus or with a hockey team. Thanks to Ballard I can do both."

The stories about Ballard are never-ending. How many are true is impossible to know, but here are some of them.*

• Ballard typically drove like a car thief who had a police cruiser on his tail. One time, his best friend, King Clancy, refused to stay in the car with Ballard because he drove too fast.

"Stop," screamed Clancy from the back seat.

Ballard ignored him.

"Stop, or I'll start a fire here in the back seat!" Clancy hollered. Still no reaction from Ballard.

Clancy set fire to a newspaper and watched the flames climb to the roof. Only then did Ballard stop. He climbed out of the car, pulled Clancy from the back seat, and drove off, leaving Clancy standing alone on the side of the highway.

• Ballard liked girls. One time, he entered a night club that had a large pool filled with bikini-clad swimmers. Ballard decided to go for a dip.

"It would be fun to get to know these girls," he shouted.

No one could talk him out of it and he was soon splashing about in the water.

---

* Quoted with permission from the author, Bill Houston, from his book, *Ballard: A Portrait of Canada's Most Controversial Sports Figure.*

• *Ballard allowed the Toronto Toros of the WHA to play in Maple Leaf Gardens at the cost of $15,000 a game. The Toros wanted to televise their games, but Ballard refused to turn on the banks of television lights.*

"There is nothing in the contract about lighting," laughed Ballard.

In the end, he agreed to hit the switch—at the cost of an extra $3,500 a night.

Harold Ballard was forever telling people that when my career ended I would have an important job with the Maple Leafs. He said it, not me. If anyone ever asked me, I always answered, "No, I won't.

Mostly I said nothing. When our children were small and the Maple Leafs' mess was at its worst, at the beginning of the eighties, I concentrated on spending time with my family and friends. I did what I could on the ice and shied away from involvement in all the other goings-on.

Ballard talked, the newspapers wrote, and I played hockey.

There has been considerable speculation about why Harold Ballard liked me so much. But even I don't know the answer. I never said anything special to him or tried to suck up to him because he was the boss. I treated him like anyone else, like another one of the guys on the team.

Maybe he appreciated that.

The only personal favor I ever did for him was to obtain a part for a garden pump. It wasn't particularly important. Ballard liked to do things his own way and to get things cheap if he could. He could have found the part for the pump in Canada, but it wasn't urgent and he thought it would be nice if I could help him.

"Hey, Börje, this damn thing is broken. When you go home for the summer, could you check if there is one like it in your country?"

I agreed. It was no big deal. I just had to find an iron-monger and buy one. When I handed it to Ballard, his face lit up.

Ballard could be cruel. He hurt a lot of people with his insensitive statements to the press. With Ballard, the reporters didn't have to exaggerate, they just had to repeat whatever Ballard said and let the scandals unfold. When he was general manager, Jim Gregory once told coach Roger Neilson: "There's a crisis a day around this place."

But personally I couldn't stay angry with Ballard and other players felt the same. Where I was concerned, he was primarily a harmless, kind old man. He would come into the dressing room to chat with the players, or some-times lecture or shout at us. He and King Clancy had a pri-vate box not far from the ice where they sat for our games, and they always came on our road trips.

The people who worked for Ballard seemed to love him or hate him. Maybe that's because there wasn't just one Harold Ballard, there were at least two. There was the soft-hearted old man who supported various charities, and the mean-spirited ogre who could be merciless in his public criticisms. When Inge and I joined the Leafs in 1973, we quickly realized that the club's owner was unique. He had just recently been released from prison where he had served time for fraud and theft.

Among other misdeeds, Ballard had been dishonest with receipts and had charged repairs done to his personal properties to Maple Leaf Gardens. From what I heard, Bal-lard could have paid a fine, but he refused to because he didn't think he had done anything wrong. So, after a judge found him guilty on 47 of 49 charges, he was sent to a minimum security institution where he drove a truck during the day and ran the Maple Leafs by telephone.

Incarceration didn't soften Ballard's outrageous style. While out on parole, he told the press that life in prison was a breeze, with steak for dinner and color television before bed.

But the 69-year-old Ballard must have been a model prisoner. He served less than one year of his three-year sentence.

After Ballard won full control of Maple Leaf Gardens in 1972, he built a small apartment inside the Gardens where he lived when he got out of prison. His wife, Dorothy, had died in 1969 and the hockey team became Ballard's life. He spent most of his time with his old friend, King Clancy. The pair was inseparable.

They were like two teenage boys who had the Maple Leafs as a hobby. King often had the task of smoothing over damage done by Ballard's harsh outbursts. It was lucky that diplomacy came naturally to King, a kind man who was friendly towards everyone.

Ballard treated King like a brother. For Clancy's 80th birthday, Ballard presented him with a 10-year contract.

"Just so you're safe in case I become senile and try to sell you," Ballard laughed, slapping Clancy on the back.

Ballard had diabetes and a heart problem, but he loved chocolate and sweets. No problem, he'd say. He just took an extra dose of insulin and continued to fill himself with goodies.

Some describe Ballard as a money-hungry capitalist, but I believe he loved hockey above everything else. He wasn't just in it for the money; hockey was his life. If anything, his burning passion for the Leafs had too much fire. Unfortunately, it was Toronto's hockey fans who got burned.

Ballard wouldn't allow anyone else to make decisions. I don't know if anyone tried in private to give him advice or challenge him, but it seemed that no one wanted to get into a public battle with Harold Ballard.

In 1978, when he was 75, Ballard bought the Hamilton Tiger-Cats of the Canadian Football League. It seemed as if he was spreading himself too thin and not concentrating enough on any one project. One day, a Ti-cat executive asked Ballard why he'd bought the team.

"If my wife were alive, I'd have done exactly what all 75-year-olds do," Ballard replied. "I'd have moved to Florida. Now this keeps me busy. When I'm busy, the nights aren't so long."

The Tiger-Cats, incidentally, added another chapter in the ongoing feud between Ballard and Alan Eagleson. To promote his new football toy, Ballard had a tiger painted on the ice at Maple Leaf Gardens. (Tiger Williams loved it. Every time he scored, he gave the tiger a kiss.)

But Eagleson objected to a rival sport being advertised at a hockey game. So they waged another battle. Over the years, Eagleson and Ballard had crossed swords over players' contracts, games against the Soviets, and several other issues. They seemed to enjoy feuding with each other. In any event, they gave the papers lots to write about.

When the WHA was fighting to get established in the 1970s, Ballard manoeuvered to make life for the Toronto Toros as difficult as possible. In the end he allowed them to rent Maple Leaf Gardens for their home games. But the rental fee was exorbitant and the Toros lasted only two seasons in Toronto. The team moved to Birmingham, Alabama, and changed its name to the Bulls.

Ballard could be unbelievably stubborn. Shortly after the Soviet Union shot down a civilian Korean aircraft in

1983, a Russian circus was scheduled for several shows at the Gardens. But Ballard would have nothing to do with it.

"It goes!" he roared. "I won't have any bloody Russians in my arena." The performances were cancelled and the circus had to pack up and move on.

During my 16 years in Toronto, the only time I had any personal contact with Ballard outside Maple Leaf Gardens was during a short vacation in the mid-'80s. The league takes an annual winter break to play the all-star game. I wasn't going to the game one year, so Margitta and I decided to take a last-minute trip to the Caribbean. Because of the late notice, however, the Gardens' travel agent said there wasn't much available.

"There are still some seats for the Cayman Islands," she said. "If you go there, you can take some cash to Mr. Ballard. He just called and asked us to send him some money."

The Caymans, not far from Jamaica, sounded like an ideal place to relax, sunbathe, and swim for a few days. That's all we wanted, so we booked the tickets and boarded the plane the next day. Before we left, we collected the envelope containing Ballard's money.

Ballard was waiting for us. As we stepped onto the tarmac, we heard his booming voice: "Börje!" He ordered a taxi and, because we were all headed in the same direction, we all climbed in. But he refused to take us to our hotel.

"Hotel? No way. You're staying with us," he roared, looking at his lady friend, Yolanda MacMillan, for approval.

We protested as best we could, but it was an awkward situation. We wanted a couple of days of peace and quiet in the sun. It's tough, however, to say no to Ballard.

"There'll be no discussion," he said. "You're staying with us and that's final."

So we cancelled our hotel and moved in with Ballard.

Actually, it turned out to be a pleasant vacation. Ballard's apartment was right by the sea and it was big enough that we didn't feel in the way.

Away from the crowds, Ballard was a different person. He wasn't noisy or bossy. We shared some hockey memories, relaxed, and ate well.

Then coach John Brophy phoned and said he wanted me to be ready to play a day early, even though I was slightly injured. I was prepared to pack up and leave, but Ballard thought it ridiculous that I should play hurt. In addition, he didn't want to lose his guest.

"Börje stays with us," he said to Brophy.

And that was that.

15

Rumor
and Cocaine

The music was loud, the beer cold, and the party in full swing. And, in keeping with the trend of the early '80s, the traffic to and from the washroom was heavy. I didn't participate myself, but I knew what was going on.

Cocaine.

I stuck to liquor or beer. I had no interest in drugs. But as the night dragged and I drank too much, I also found myself rolling up a dollar bill. I was drunk. I wasn't thinking clearly. I sniffed a couple of lines of cocaine.

I got high that night, but the next day I was in agony. The after-effects were like nothing I'd ever experienced. The suffering is difficult to describe, but it was far worse than a bad hangover. It was awful and I decided at once never to do it again. And I didn't.

Many years later, I admitted sampling cocaine to a reporter from the *Toronto Star*. I spoke up after a story in *Sports Illustrated* alleged that some Edmonton players used cocaine. Following that article, rumors began to spread about me and cocaine. I decided to confront them head on. Edmonton's players were considered by some to be farm boys who couldn't cope with life in the big city. According to the gossip, they sniffed cocaine when they visited New York and other "in" cities. The rumors about me developed because of my long history of sinus trouble.

The rumor mongers added two and two together, but got five. They pointed out that the Leafs were playing poorly, Salming has sinus problems, and athletes some-times use cocaine. Therefore, Salming is on the stuff.

I disliked talking about this, but what could I do? The rumors were eating me up. Talking about my sinus woes sounds like a convenient alibi. But anyone who knows me is aware that I have had trouble with my sinuses since I was a child. All the years of sweating in cold arenas, then showering and stepping out onto winter streets can't have helped my condition. But, as I said, all this sounds like an excuse.

The rumors made my life difficult for a while. My family and I felt that we were being accused. We knew the truth, but that wasn't enough to stop the gossip or the stares, or to silence my children's schoolmates.

This comparison is perhaps lame, but I have tried snuff and don't use it, have tried cigarettes but don't smoke, and have tried cocaine but don't use drugs. It is that simple. The whole incident was nothing more serious than a quick experiment. It was stupid, of course, something I'd never recommend. But what more can I say?

The rumors flew wildly. I suppose that's the price of being a hockey celebrity. A Mr. Smith can go crazy sever-al times a year and no one cares. But I can hardly piss in the forest without stories being written about how I caused a flood.

After the *Sports Illustrated* story, I felt I had to set the record straight. So when a local reporter called and asked for an interview, I decided to tell her about the party many years earlier.

The reporter came to my home and got straight to the point:

"Do you use cocaine?"

"No."

"Have you used cocaine?"

"Yes, I've tried it. It was at a party in 1980. I'm not very proud about it."

"So it was a one-time experiment?"

"Yes. It wasn't very clever of me, especially as everyone's eyes are on me. Cocaine is awful. I object to everything that drugs represent."

I don't know if the journalist misunderstood what I meant by "drugs." I meant illegal drugs because that was what we were talking about. But the newspaper read that I also objected to alcohol.

Maybe the reporter thought she was doing me a favor. To suggest, however, that I don't drink is untrue. I have never tried to hide the fact that, like most people, I have a drink occasionally. That's nothing to be ashamed of. I am no angel. In any event, there was a terrible uproar.

The Maple Leafs management called me in for questioning. The NHL wanted to suspend me. This all happened in the summer of 1986, so it was an old event that caused my suffering. The NHL has always taken a hard line against drug use. My case wasn't helped that summer by newspaper accounts of the death of a football player from an overdose, and stories about a basketball star who was battling a cocaine problem. There was pressure on the NHL to take a tough stand.

NHL president John Ziegler summoned me to New York for a hearing. I flew there with lawyers from the Maple Leafs. I met with Ziegler in his Manhattan office.

"Mr. Salming, this is not very good for you or the NHL," he said.

I told my story again, but I understood that Ziegler's position was difficult. I didn't think I should be suspended for an offence that I hadn't even been obliged to disclose, particularly an offence that had been committed six years earlier. So I pleaded my case.

"I'm 35," I began. "I have a wife and two children. I live to play hockey, which I couldn't do if I used drugs, certainly not for this many years. You can test me if you like."

Ziegler explained that the NHL was committed to a policy of zero-toleration of drugs. He was forced to suspend me. I sat out a total of eight games. At the time, I had sympathy for Ziegler's position. I felt a bit like a scapegoat, but I could understand why Ziegler felt obliged to use me to send a loud warning across the league.

Today I have a different opinion. I think the NHL's drug policy is completely wrong because it is entirely punitive. There is no room for understanding or help, if it's needed. Any player found using drugs is kicked out of the league, which can be a devastating blow. Why not help the guy instead?

The NHL has a good internal security department that informs players about drugs, alcohol, and the general risks of keeping bad company. Before each season, the security personnel visit every team to dispense their good advice and to distribute telephone numbers of helpful contacts across the league.

There are qualified professionals to contact if a player encounters blackmail or has a problem with alcohol. But there is no help for anyone who develops a problem with cocaine.

Many of the young players entering the NHL today receive incredible contracts. The risk is high that these impressionable young men will attract disreputable people, sleazy characters who are pulled towards someone else's fame and wealth like sharks to blood.

"Hey, man, get in on this deal. It's easy money."

I've heard all the lines. It sometimes isn't easy for a young player to know when to say no. Perhaps he'll innocently tag along to a big party and find himself in a room full of strangers who are connected with who knows what kinds of trouble.

Whether the NHL likes it or not, some illicit drugs are as common in North American society as alcohol. Hockey players are no different from the next guy. They find themselves in all types of situations and occasionally they make wrong decisions.

The pressures and temptations can be particularly great for a young, promising player whose NHL career gets off to a rocky start. He is often far from home, in an unfamiliar city, coping as well as he can with a new life in a harsh, demanding league. Management, teammates, fans, and even the player himself fashion an atmosphere of high expectation. In this climate, a young player can be extremely vulnerable.

The NHL should have resources to help players discreetly who find themselves on the wrong track. Suspending them is no solution. More helpful for everyone would be programs of consultation and rehabilitation.

The rumors about me reached back to Sweden and had repercussions on my place on the national team. I was in line for the 1985 world championship team and would have gladly played.

But federation captain Leif Boork rejected me because he had heard that I used drugs. He never called to ask me about the rumors directly, or to let me explain how the stories got started.

When you have a high public profile, wild rumors seem inevitably to follow. Most are without any foundation and become more fantastic each time they're told. Sometimes, an unprofessional journalist will hear something from someone who has heard something from a friend, and suddenly it appears as fact in a newspaper. Once a story like that gets out, it's almost impossible to disprove.

I could understand if Boork had rejected me because I wasn't good enough, but to pass me over because he suspected I used drugs was totally unfair. It reached the point in Sweden that my alleged habit was discussed at coaching seminars that Stig attended.

One day, he called to ask me directly about the rumors.

"What are you up to, really?" he asked.

He was worried about me, and wanted to hear the truth. Living so far apart from me, it was difficult for Stig to know how much credence to give the stories circulating in Sweden. It bothered me that even Stig had doubts about his younger brother.

Today, I have no regrets that I spoke up about my one-night stand with cocaine. It upset me to be suspended for telling the truth, but in the end it was worth it. I finally got a chance to tell the real story.

As far as hockey was concerned, the entire 1980s were lacking in vision and success for the Maple Leafs. Controversy and mud throwing seemed to occur almost daily. The players never knew what to expect next. But, despite everything, I decided to stay if the money was right and the club wanted me. I would do my job.

Anders and Teresa were settled in school in Toronto. They had their friends and we had our friends outside hockey. My family came first. I just kept hoping that the club would eventually stumble on better times. But the good times never arrived. Coaches came and went. We kept bringing in young, talented players and were often called a promising team, but we never went anywhere. Even so, the public kept filling the Gardens. Toronto fans are really fantastic.

I think they understood the situation, and understood how I felt about everything. They seemed to respect that I refused to get dragged into the circus. I'm grateful for that. But it wasn't easy to operate in that atmosphere of hopelessness.

My strength to persevere through the difficult times came from Margitta, my strong partner through all the years. She was at my side in 1973 when I first landed in Toronto, and remained there through the good years and the bad. I am no unemotional superman who stoically accepted all the stupidity that poisoned the team. Often, I was consumed by a deep sense of frustration and helplessness.

During those times, Margitta offered her shoulder for me to cry on. Without her, I don't know if I could have endured the long, losing years in Toronto. She has always been there when I needed support.

At the beginning of my NHL career, various teammates lived near our home in Mississauga. But over the years, as players were traded away, it became difficult for both Margitta and me to stay in contact with friends who were forced to move several thousand kilometres.

During the season, at least I had hockey, travelling, and my teammates; Margitta was forced to spend most of her time at home, particularly when the children were small. It must have been lonely in the suburbs, but she took courses and pursued her great interest in art and design. She also got help with babysitting and other day-to-day matters from wonderful neighbors. In particular, we became good friends with the Harvey family.

For the first few years, Margitta was my English teacher. Even before coming to Canada, Margitta's English was solid, but she still enrolled in courses to perfect her speech. Her acumen proved advantageous for me. It became a bit much to keep pointing at signs and using sign language.

Outside our home, most of the English I learned came from the dressing room. But hockey players place little emphasis on precise grammar and polite vocabulary. I picked up a lot of four-letter words, which came in handy at the rink, but were of little use when I strolled into the real world. I needed more than profanities and slang. Luckily, I had Margitta. Patiently, she instructed me, correcting my imperfect pronunciations and rough grammar.

After a few years in Mississauga, we grew tired of the suburbs and moved to the High Park district of Toronto, closer to the core of the city. We could get downtown on public transit in 25 minutes.

After a year back in Sweden, we haven't longed to return to Toronto. Sweden is our home now, although our memories of Toronto are fond. We had a cozy, old house and enjoyed the city; we'll undoubtedly visit often.

Toronto lies beside Lake Ontario. It has public beaches and, in the summer, the lake is filled with windsurfers, sailboats, and fishermen. Toronto abounds with good restaurants and is ideal for cycling and taking long walks. The city is also safe and clean. I am shocked at all the graffiti in Sweden; it is almost non-existent in Toronto.

It is a cosmopolitan city, combining different cultures from around the world. Each ethnic group has its own shops and restaurants, making it possible for someone to eat around the world without leaving the city. Toronto is also big enough (about three million residents) to attract the world's best performers and artists. Concerts and exhibitions of all type are common. The newest concert site is the SkyDome, a 50,000-seat stadium with a retractable roof that was built primarily for baseball. The Toronto Blue Jays, the major-league ball team, regularly attract a full house.

Hockey people had better be vigilant that coming generations don't turn from their first love, hockey, to baseball.

16

Pills, Knives and Visors

Over the years, doctors have sewn hundreds of stitches to repair the dozens of cuts that Börje has suffered. We tried to count them all, but it was impossible. There have been the small cuts here and there, courtesy of a high stick or a deflected puck, the usual gashes received by all hockey players. And there have been serious, career-threatening injuries.

After considerable reflection, we compiled the following medical ledger for our hockey patient, Börje Salming:

Forehead: Stitched eight or nine times.

Nose: Broken five times, stitched and straightened several times.

Eyebrows: Stitched more than 20 times.

Right eye: 50% loss of sight from a high stick. Scar extending from the forehead over the eye to the corner of the mouth.

Left eye: Slightly injured by a high stick.

Left ear: Ear lobe stitched.

Mouth: Five teeth knocked out, bridge.

Chin: Stitched 10 to 15 times.
Ribs: Broken.
Lungs: One punctured.
Shoulders: Dislocated twice.
Elbows: Broken several times, loose chips.
Right hand: Four broken fingers. Crushed thumb.
Legs: Hemorrhages, muscle pulls.
Knees: Cracked knee cap. Cartilage removed.
Feet: Cracked left heel.
Ankles: Stitched three times.

This list isn't pleasant reading, but, despite everything, I'd say I've been lucky. Spread out over all the hours I spent on the ice, my injuries haven't been so terrible.

My most serious injury occurred during the 1978 quarter-finals against the Islanders. I was carrying the puck and tried to cut behind Lorne Henning. As I tried to shoot, he spun around to hook me and accidentally struck my eye with his stick.

The pain was excruciating. When the point of his blade stabbed my eye, I felt as if my eye was going to come out the back of my head. My nose was broken and I was bleeding into my sinuses. The trainer laid me down on the bench and I promptly vomited blood all over the place. The sight must have been gruesome. By the time I reached the hospital, the pain was driving me crazy.

"Painkillers! Give me painkillers!" I screamed.

But the doctor was reluctant to give me too much medication because the seriousness of the injury meant that surgery was likely. I have no real recollection of these hours, other than the memory that my head seemed to be splitting.

My eyes were bandaged, and no one knew for certain if I'd ever regain use of my battered right eye. A day passed.

Then two. Margitta was beside herself with worry. Would I lose the eye? If so, my hockey career would be finished.

The hospital staff was wonderful and my doctor remained calm.

"Lucky that you have such a big nose," he joked as he removed the bandages to examine my eye.

"This type of injury usually heals," he said. "But there's a risk that your vision will be impaired."

He shone a light into my pupil and examined me carefully.

"Take a look in the mirror, then you'll be blind for a week," he said. "I have to bandage both eyes so that your right eye is completely rested."

I went to the mirror. The eye was completely red—not just the white area, but the pupil as well.

During the next seven days, I learned how it felt to be blind and totally reliant on other people. I could do nothing by myself. Even finding my plate when I wanted to eat was a challenge.

The bandages eventually came off and the prognosis was optimistic. I'd had a close call, but I was able to resume my career after the summer.

A defenceman's ankles are extremely vulnerable. I have a painful memory of one hard shot I blocked with an ankle during a routine game. It hurt, but, instead of leaving the game, my ankle was frozen with my skate still laced up. It is imperative to keep the skate on because as soon as it is untied the ankle swells and it becomes impossible to squeeze it back into the boot. At home that night, the pain was unbearable. It was impossible to sleep so, at about 4 a.m., I crept downstairs to the kitchen medicine cabinet. Margitta and the children were sleeping. I tore open the cabinet door, grabbed two or three bottles of pills, and swallowed a handful of tablets. I took far more than the recommended dosage, but at that point all I cared about was easing the pain.

Another time, alone in a Detroit hotel room early one November morning, my eyes welled with tears as I stared into the mirror.

"Oh, my God," I stammered. "Am I going to look like this for the rest of my life?"

The previous night, my face had been split open by the skate blade of Red Wings' forward Gerard Gallant. Again, it was an accident, but one that could have changed my life. Today, I can joke about how once again my sight was saved by my big nose. But on that awful morning all I saw was the face of a badly disfigured man.

The incident happened during a scramble in front of our goal. I fell, and a second later Gallant was pushed from behind. His skate came down on my face. The cold steel sliced the skin above my right eye, then cut deeply into my nose and along the side of my face. It's odd, but there was no more pain than cutting a finger with a sharp knife. I knew that something serious had happened, but the cut was so fast and clean, it didn't hurt. I got up on my own and skated off the ice. When I reached our bench, my knees buckled and the other players had to help me lie down.

The trainer, Guy Kinnear, tried to stop the bleeding with a towel, but the blood soaked right through.

"Get more towels!" Kinnear screamed to his assistant, Dan Lemelin.

Only then did I begin to understand the seriousness of the situation. I saw the blood. It was everywhere and still gushing. Then the pain set in.

Carefully, I was carried to the infirmary, where I was

examined by a doctor. He took one look at me and announced, "Get him to the hospital."

Minor cuts are stitched right at the arena. I'd undergone that procedure many times: a local anesthetic, a quick stitching job, and back to the ice. But this latest wound required the expert hand of a specialist. I was lucky to fall under the care of Dr. John Finley. The first thing he did when I reached the hospital was to calm me down.

"This isn't serious," he said. "You'll be all right."

While Dr. Finley changed into his surgical gown, nurses prepared me for the operating table. Then Dr. Finley went to work. I was awake for the entire procedure and could see the tiny hook pricking my skin.

After what seemed like an eternity, I asked, "Almost done?"

"Young man," said the doctor, "we've just left second base."

Second base is only halfway home. The stitching began at 11 p.m. and lasted until two in the morning.

I returned by ambulance to our hotel and the driver took me to my room in a wheelchair. To control the swelling, I had a pressure bandage over my face. I collapsed into bed, exhausted by the long night and drowsy from the morphine.

In the morning, I removed the pressure bandage in front of the mirror, and had to sit down in a chair. Nearly 300 stitches crisscrossed my forehead, ran past my eye, across my nose, back under the eye, down the length of my cheek, and ended at the corner of my mouth. Black threads poked out everywhere and my hair was matted with dried blood.

I showered for a long time, watching the blood disappear down the drain. The shower made me feel better and

I even looked slightly better without all the dried blood. The doctor had done a fine job. I lifted the phone and called Margitta. It wasn't easy describing my appearance, but I wanted her to be prepared before I arrived home.

It felt awful to be so disfigured. People stared when I arrived at the Detroit airport. I wanted the plane to leave at once, but I had to wait in the departure lounge. I shielded my face with a newspaper to deflect the gawking.

It was difficult for a long time, but eventually we realized that the doctor had done a superb job. The red snake of a scar became smaller and smaller, until it nearly disappeared altogether. Dr. Finley, quite simply, had done wonderful work.

Years later, I bumped into the captain who had piloted me home to Toronto on the morning after the injury.

"I can hardly believe it's the same guy," he said, marvelling at the doctor's handiwork.

My injury in Detroit would have been much less serious if I hadn't been so stubborn about attaching a visor to my helmet. A week earlier, I had had to use a visor after taking a couple of stitches above my eyebrow. But I discarded it after a few practices, and lived to regret my decision in Detroit.

I have always preferred to use the minimum amount of equipment. Too much padding restricts mobility and weighs you down. The trainers probably never liked the way I'd take a knife and cut away at the various pieces of protective gear.

Originally, I disliked visors because they fogged up. But they've improved over the years and I've come to realize that it's worth it to protect yourself. But sometimes even the best equipment is insufficient. Once, I blocked a hard shot with my knee cap. The pain was terrible but I continued the game. Afterwards, however, X-rays showed that the knee cap was cracked. The doctor was astounded that I'd played with the injury.

Sometimes I ask myself if all the pain and injuries are worth it. The answer is always yes. Overall, I have coped quite well. Perhaps my durability can be traced back to my tough childhood. I learned to endure a lot of punishment and accept hard work. My body became resilient. It takes the blows and recovers quickly.

As a child, I had hours of rigorous, natural training. I'm not talking about athletic training, but about the long forest walks to go fishing in the mountains, the rowing trips, the strenuous cycling tours, and the tedious hours spent working in a sand and gravel pit outside Gävle. My muscles were strengthened easily and naturally. It's helped, too, that I've never had a serious knee injury. Once a hockey player's knees start to go, his days are numbered.

The natural body building of my youth is probably better than pushing a teenager into a gym to build his muscles suddenly through hard work. I'm not suggesting that weight training is a waste of time, only that my various childhood activities meant that I never had to lift weights myself. My body was sculptured for an athletic career in a gradual, natural way. I never had to think about getting in shape; it just happened.

My only enduring physical problem was my inflamed sinuses. Over the years, I've visited several doctors and taken all kinds of medication. No penicillin exists that I haven't tried. At one time in my life, I felt like a human guinea pig. I tried just about everything, but nothing helped permanently. I've tried various remedies, gone into hospital for week-long treatments, and had my sinuses scraped by doctors a couple of times. But any improvement was only temporary.

159

I was forever catching colds and fevers. For a long time, I had persistent pain through my forehead and nose, and endured a light but continuous headache.

I received dozens of remedies from friendly people who wanted to help me get well. If I had tested them all, I wouldn't have had time for anything else. I did, however, look into some of them. That's how I found the answer—acupuncture.

Through Dr. Neal, the chiropractor, I contacted a Toronto acupuncturist in 1979. I usually call him the old Japanese guy, but that name is a disservice to the amazing work of Dr. Harry Nishimoto. We met when he was the sprightly age of 74. He soon had me feeling better.

Dr. Nishimoto's treatments eased the pressure over my forehead and nose. I found it easier to breathe when exercising. I also caught fewer colds. The treatment works by using tiny acupuncture needles to stimulate blood circulation and help the body's own immune system to work more effectively.

Occasionally, over the years, I played when I shouldn't have. But those who have criticized coaches for using me too much should know that I like to play a lot. When I was young and healthy, I wanted to play 35 minutes a game. Sometimes, though, I played as much as 45 minutes, even if I wasn't up to it.

Some days, it became too much. The more I played, the worse my sinuses got and I nearly always had a cold. On one occasion, during the 1980-81 season, while Punch Imlach was running the club, I had to stop; my body couldn't take any more.

I was taken to hospital, where doctors prescribed intravenous penicillin and a week in bed. Imlach was not pleased. The team was short a defenceman for an important game as the Leafs were battling Quebec for a playoff spot. It was the only thing that Imlach cared about.

The day before the game, the doctor appeared at my bedside and told me that Imlach was on the phone.

"He wants you to play tomorrow," the doctor said. "He has already spoken to me and I refused. There is no way you should play."

Then the doctor handed me the receiver.

"Hello, Börje," Imlach began. "You know how important this game is. We need you."

"I'm lying here with tubes in my arms," I replied. "Try to understand. The doctor forbids me to play. So, no, I can't do it."

"Don't worry," Imlach said. "We'll come up and get you. It'll only be for a couple of hours. Then we'll take you right back to the hospital after the game."

"No, I can't," I said.

The next sound I heard was Imlach slamming down the phone.

———

I also want to thank the doctors of the Toronto Maple Leafs: Dr. Hastings, Dr. Douglas, Dr. Urowitz, Dr. McGrail and Dr. Easterbrook. They were all wonderful and also became my good friends.

17

Home Again

When Börje returned to Sweden and signed with AIK in 1990, most hockey observers regarded it as little more than a public relations coup for the Stockholm team.

But Anders Hedberg, the club's director, saw it as something more, and he was right.

The mere presence of Börje Salming raised the level of play among the younger players, and Börje himself dominated many games. He wasn't a has-been professional. He was the motor that propelled the whole team. In the regular season games before Christmas, AIK finished in fourth place.

I wouldn't have stayed with the Maple Leafs so long if not for our fondness for Toronto and all the friends we'd made there. But maybe we waited too long before coming home. I don't know.

When I left Sweden in 1973, the NHL was meant to be a temporary stop. I intended to build an economic foundation for the future and then move back to Sweden. But I stayed in Canada for 17 years.

Margitta and I thought a lot about coming home during the last few years. But the children were happy and we didn't want to take them away from their school and their friends. We also wanted to ensure that they had a strong grasp of English.

During my last year with the Leafs, there was considerable speculation about which team I would join to end my career. But, as far as I was concerned, the only possibilities were Buffalo and Detroit. I was determined to remain within commuting distance of Toronto.

The Detroit Red Wings offered me generous conditions, both in money and time off to visit my family in Toronto. So, I went to Detroit for my final NHL season. I hope they were happy with the job I did, even though the team had a disappointing year.

Now Margitta and I, in our fortieth years, are home again, with an exciting and eventful phase of our life behind us. But the future feels equally exciting, although as uncertain as the day, so many years ago, when we moved into the Westbury Hotel beside Maple Leaf Gardens.

The summer and autumn of 1990 were hectic and confusing. We lived out of a suitcase for six months. We had some belongings in Toronto, some with family in Waxholm, and some in our summer home outside Gävle. Everything finally sorted itself out, however, and the move has gone fairly smoothly, thanks mainly to Margitta's sister, Anna-Lena, and her husband, Kent. We lived with them for all of the fall, until we found a house of our own in the same neighborhood. It worked out perfectly for the children, who had already started school in Waxholm and didn't have to change once we moved. I was away so long that I have trouble remembering some Swedish words, but it won't take long before they come back to me.

Everyone here has been so kind to us. Anders Hedberg and AIK have really tried to make our homecoming smooth.

Teresa and Anders have already made new friends and are taking special lessons in Swedish. They have adjusted well, which is important. They seem happy to be completing their schooling in Sweden. If someday they want to move back, Toronto will always be there.

Anders was offered a spot with AIK's juniors, but I was reluctant to send him into the limelight. He'll play instead for the local club. Still, we understand that he will always be a Salming, always expected to be something more than just another player. It doesn't seem right that he will always be compared to me. He is his own person. But we can't change people's attitudes. Anyway, he may choose a life outside of hockey. He'll have to make that decision for himself.

Some people think I was crazy to return to Sweden's elite division. But there were many reasons for my decision. We wanted to live in Stockholm because we have become city people, and we have family here. Also, I still want to play hockey and saw this opportunity as both fun and challenging. Playing hockey will give me a chance to meet many people and make new friends. After 17 years on the other side of the Atlantic, we don't have many Swedish friends.

I made my decision during the 1989 world championships, which were played in Stockholm. Returning to the larger European ice surface was a refreshing change. I enjoyed it. And, as I've already mentioned, I prefer the Swedish style of coaching to that practised by many loud-mouthed former players in the NHL. In Sweden, coaches use constructive criticism and challenging, imaginative practices to help players improve.

Our coaches at AIK, Leif Holmgren and Thomas Gradin, are part of the team but retain enough authority and distance to be our leaders. In the NHL, there was a lot of authority and distance, but little practical knowledge or effective training.

Even at my age, I've learned new things during my season at home. I'm hoping that I can return the favor by teaching the young players some of the lessons I've picked up along the way. It feels good. At first, some of my teammates were tentative around me. I think my reputation made them nervous. But, in time, this exaggerated respect faded and now I'm treated like one of the team.

I can understand how my teammates must have felt in the beginning. I felt the same way when I started in the NHL and met the superstars I'd read about in the papers. But I just want to be one of the guys.

One thing I've had to get used to is the comments I get now that I'm approaching middle age. For instance, as fans lined up for autographs after a game in Gothenburg, AIK teammate Peter Hammarström turned to me and said, "When I was a little boy, I once lined up like that to get your autograph." Clearly, I'm quite a bit older than most of my teammates.

The larger ice surfaces make hockey more fun here than in Canada. European rinks are five metres wider than the standard NHL surface. As a defenceman, I have more time to make a play, more room to skate, and more opportunity to avoid a bodycheck.

But while European hockey is more fun to play, the Canadian brand is more fun to watch. The smaller rinks encourage more physical contact. The game is more emotional and more hectic. I think crowds like that. They want lots of action. So do I—when I'm a spectator.

So what will happen when I finally hang up my skates? I wonder.

Perhaps I will become a consultant for an equipment manufacturer. I've had plenty of offers. Over the years, I often took a knife and remodeled my own equipment, cutting away excess padding or contouring my gear to make it more flexible and comfortable. I have a few tips that would be useful.

Thanks to the shorter road trips and condensed playing schedule, I have more spare time now than at any time in my career. I don't accept every invitation I receive, but I have agreed to try a few new projects, activities I always refused in the past. For example, I have been visiting schools to speak out against vandalism and graffiti. So far, I've enjoyed talking to the kids. Maybe when I have more time, I'll become even more involved.

The one mistake I won't make is to rush headlong into something new and become so busy that I have no time for my family. I owe it to Margitta and our two children to take it easy for a while and to support them as they supported me during my long career.

They have always been there for me. Now I want to be there for them.

Swedish Hockey

by Gerhard Karlsson

Ice hockey is a relatively young sport in Sweden. But after its definite breakthrough in 1949, with the World Cup in Stockholm, hockey has overtaken the more traditional Swedish sports such as skiing and bandy* in popularity. Today, hockey is clearly the leading spectator sport, while an earlier crowd pleaser, soccer, struggles to attract an audience.

Swedish hockey games in the elite series attract an average of 6,000 fans per match, full capacity for most arenas. The number of spectators has increased in recent years, and it is no exaggeration to call ice hockey the national sport of Sweden.

All Swedish hockey players are called amateurs, but this is a qualified truth. An absolutely top player (for example,

---

* Bandy combines ice hockey and soccer. It is played on a field of ice that is as large as a soccer field. Each team has eleven players, including the goalkeeper. The players use short, bent clubs and play with a little red ball.

a professional returned home from the NHL) can earn $15,000 per month on a big city team that has good fan support (Stockholm, Gothenburg, and Malmö). However, this amount is rare. The average salary in the elite series is about $4,500 per month, ranging from $365 to $15,000.

Within Swedish sport, there is talk of "social responsibility" for those active at the top level. The idea is that job training or a job should be offered to a player during his playing days to prepare him for the day when his career is over. This goal is reached fairly often, but not always. Some clubs attract young players with fat contracts and offer considerably less for the future.

Young players live well from hockey and forget to think about their lives 20 years down the road. Still, hockey teams usually succeed quite well in producing skillful young players and, later, well-balanced, "pensioned" athletes.

Börje Salming paved the way for the Swedish exodus to the NHL. He was the first to be really successful and to show that Swedes were not necessarily "chicken." Börje's and other Swedes' success in the NHL during the 1970s frightened the Swedish Hockey Federation who feared that Swedish teams would be gutted. Fortunately, their misgivings did not materialize. The dream of playing in the NHL has encouraged many more youngsters to play hockey seriously, and today a balance exists between good, young players who stay in Sweden and those who leave for a few years in the NHL.

As well, fewer players today jump at the first good contract offered. Young Swedes used to go over to North America without having the mental or physical strength to cope with the tough matches and the atmosphere that prevails in the NHL. Today, the majority of young players who are offered professional contracts choose to spend several years playing in the Swedish elite series. They also gain international experience by playing for the national team, Tre Kronor.

Salming was the first to do well, but he was not the first Swedish player in the NHL. A legend in Sweden in the '50s and '60s, Sven Tumba played professionally for the Boston Bruins in 1958 and scored a celebrated goal in a 2-2 game against the Rangers. But he didn't like the small rinks or the hard play, so he refused the contract he was offered and returned to Sweden where he continued to be a star for many years.

Ulf Sterner was the first Swede to sign with an NHL club. In Sweden he was known as a fighter and a tough forward but, as a Ranger, he was hounded and played only five games before being sent down to the farm team. Swedish hockey people were amazed that not even Sterner was tough enough for the NHL. They figured the NHL must be made up of gangsters, not athletes.

Juha Widing grew up in Sweden and played hockey in Gothenburg. He moved to the US with his parents and later became a professional with the Rangers (1969) and then Los Angeles. At that time, Sweden had no players in the NHL and we gladly claimed Widing as our own.

In 1972, Thommie Bergman became the first Swede to play a whole season in the NHL. He negotiated a contract for himself with the Detroit Red Wings and was an adequate, big, strong defender. The next year Börje Salming and Inge Hammarström signed with the Maple Leafs, and the avalanche began. By 1991, about 120 Swedes had tried their luck in the NHL or the WHA.

Ice hockey was introduced to Sweden just after 1910, and in 1922 the Swedish Ice Hockey Federation was formed. For the first ten years, hockey existed in the shadow of soccer and bandy, but public interest gradually grew.

The sport finally captured the public's attention in 1949 when Canada, represented by the Sudbury Wolves, met Sweden in the World Cup. People flocked to the Stockholm Stadium to watch. The token police force could not control the excited crowds and, in the end, the riot barriers gave way. Eighteen people were taken to hospital by ambulance.

Today, Sweden has 224 arenas and approximately 750 clubs. The clubs themselves have both junior and senior teams, but in recent years several elite clubs have reached agreements with smaller clubs in lower divisions to use them as farm teams. Transfers between clubs cannot take place during a season. A player must represent his club for a whole season.

The elite series consists of twelve teams. Eight make the playoffs for the Swedish Gold Cup in the spring, and each team plays a total of about 50 games. Below the elite series are divisions I, II, and III. The teams climb up the divisions through a fairly complicated qualification system with playoff matches. No team in the elite series is guaranteed its place. The two worst teams must requalify for the next season or be relegated to division I.

Internationally, Sweden has always been one step behind the giant to the east, the Soviet Union. On the few occasions when Sweden has beaten the USSR, the joy among hockey fans has been enormous. During the last few years, the disparity between the teams has diminished, and when Sweden again won the World Cup in 1991, you could say that the two best teams in Europe are equal. Whether this is due to Sweden improving or to disturbances in the Soviet Union is hard to say. Probably both are true. Sweden has improved, thanks to a stimulating "relationship" with the NHL, and the Soviet Union lost strength because of growing political and ethnic problems.

While the Soviet Union has dominated European hockey for a long time, both Sweden and Czechoslovakia are catching up, closely followed by Finland. The four are in a class of their own in Europe. Germany holds the middle ground, followed by the others who have national teams. Germany concentrates mostly on its professional league in which many Swedes work as coaches. Switzerland also has a professional league that pays well, and many Swedes have chosen to play in it rather than going over to the NHL.

Sweden has won the World Cup five times: 1953 (Switzerland), 1957 (Moscow), 1962 (Colorado), 1987 (Vienna) and 1991 (Finland).

A Short
NHL Glossary

Some common hockey names and terms are defined below:

Agent: Someone who represents a player during negotiations with his club. In North America, there are many agencies that concentrate entirely on hockey.

All-Star Game: The first All-Star game in the NHL was played in 1947. A team of the best players from the rest of the League defeated Toronto 4-3. It is now traditional to hold All-Star games in the middle of the season. In 1975, All-Star games between the Wales and Campbell Conferences were introduced. Börje Salming was chosen eight times but played only four.

All-Star Team: Since 1930, the press has nominated the first and second All-Star Teams at the end of the season.

Börje Salming was chosen six times:

	First Team	Second Team
1974-75	Bernie Parent	Rogatien Vachon
	Bobby Orr	Guy Lapointe
	Denis Potvin	Börje Salming
	Bobby Clarke	Phil Esposito
	Guy Lafleur	Rene Robert
	Richard Martin	Steve Vickers
1975-76	Ken Dryden	Glenn Resch
	Denis Potvin	Börje Salming
	Brad Park	Guy Lapointe
	Bobby Clarke	Gilbert Perreault
	Guy Lafleur	Reggie Leach
	Bill Barber	Richard Martin
1976-77	Ken Dryden	Rogatien Vachon
	Larry Robinson	Denis Potvin
	Börje Salming	Guy Lapointe
	Marcel Dionne	Gilbert Perreault
	Guy Lafleur	Lanny McDonald
	Steve Shutt	Richard Martin
1977-78	Ken Dryden	Don Edwards
	Denis Potvin	Larry Robinson
	Brad Park	Börje Salming
	Bryan Trottier	Darryl Sittler
	Guy Lafleur	Mike Bossy
	Clark Gillies	Steve Shutt

1978-79	Ken Dryden	Glenn Resch
	Denis Potvin	Börje Salming
	Larry Robinson	Serge Savard
	Bryan Trottier	Marcel Dionne
	Guy Lafleur	Mike Bossy
	Clark Gillies	Bill Barber
1979-80	Tony Esposito	Don Edwards
	Larry Robinson	Börje Salming
	Raymond Bourque	Jim Schoenfeld
	Marcel Dionne	Wayne Gretzky
	Guy Lafleur	Danny Gare
	Charlie Simmer	Steve Shutt

The number of times players have been chosen for the All-Star Team looks like this:

Gordie Howe, 21	Pierre Pilote, 8
Maurice Richard, 14	Frank Brimsek, 8
Bobby Hull, 12	Mike Bossy, 8
Doug Harvey, 11	Denis Potvin, 7
Glenn Hall, 11	Brad Park, 7
Wayne Gretzky, 11	Paul Coffey, 7
Ray Bourque, 11	Jacques Plante, 7
Jean Belliveau, 10	Bill Gadsby, 7
Earl Seibert, 10	Terry Sawchuk, 7
Bobby Orr, 9	Bill Durnan, 6
Ted Lindsey, 9	Guy Lafleur, 6
Frank Mahovlich, 9	Ken Dryden, 6
Eddie Shore, 8	Larry Robinson, 6
Stan Mikita, 8	Tim Horton, 6
Red Kelly, 8	Börje Salming, 6

American Hockey League (AHL): A minor league made up of farm teams to the NHL clubs.

Bonus: Every club has a bonus system for its players. Players earn money depending on the number of goals they score, the number of games they play, how far the club goes in the playoffs, etc. In addition, many players have additional bonus clauses written into their contracts.

Coach: Responsible for team training, player choices, strategy, motivation, and leadership. The head coach often has assistant coaches to help him.

Contract: A written agreement between a player and a club. Contracts can be unique but, in practice, there are several standard alternatives. See *One-way Contract, Two-way Contract*.

Draft: When an NHL club claims the rights to a certain player. There are two types of draft: the entry draft and the waiver draft. The entry draft takes place in June when the NHL clubs meet to draft young, promising players. The season's worst team chooses first, the second worst second, and so on, for several rounds. Any player over eighteen from around the world can be drafted. Several hundred players are drafted every year, but experience shows that only those drafted in the first or second rounds can be relatively sure of an NHL contract.

The waiver draft is more complicated. Players with contracts are protected or left unprotected by their clubs. Only unprotected players can be chosen by another club. The selection order is the same as in the entry draft. When a club claims an unprotected player, it must then transfer a protected player to unprotected status. A team that loses a player and does not choose another receives economic compensation.

Franchise: Licence or right. The rights of a team to play in the NHL are regulated by a franchise agreement. An owner can sell the rights to anyone else, including a buyer in another city, but the NHL must approve the deal.

Free Agent: A player who is not claimed by any NHL club, often a young player who hasn't been drafted or an older player who has not renewed his contract with his original club.

General Manager (GM): Executive director of an NHL club. The GM is responsible for the club's business and financial direction and often acts as a link between the owner and the team. GMs are often former coaches or players.

International Hockey League (IHL): A minor league made up of farm teams to the NHL clubs.

Line-up: A list of the players who start a game.

Minor Leagues (Minors): Professional leagues made up of teams connected with NHL clubs. There are 23 teams in the minors divided into two leagues, the American Hockey League and the International Hockey League.

National Hockey League (NHL): North American ice hockey league established on November 26, 1917, in

Montreal. It comprised the following teams: Montreal
Canadiens, Montreal Wanderers, Ottawa Senators, and
Quebec Bulldogs. Later in the same year, the Toronto
Arenas joined the new league. Teams came and went but,
by 1942, the number stabilized at 6: Montreal Canadiens,
Toronto Maple Leafs, Boston Bruins, New York Rangers,
Chicago Black Hawks, and Detroit Red Wings. Beginning
in 1967, the League expanded rapidly. By 1991, the NHL
comprised 21 teams who play a schedule of 80 games a
season. Further expansion is planned for 1992.

The NHL is split into the Campbell Conference and
Wales Conference, which in turn are split into a total of
four divisions:

Campbell Conference
Norris Division:
Chicago, Detroit, Minnesota, St. Louis, Toronto.

Smythe Division:
Calgary, Edmonton, Los Angeles, Winnipeg, Vancouver.

Wales Conference
Adams Division:
Boston, Buffalo, Hartford, Montreal, Quebec.

Patrick Division:
New Jersey, New York Islanders, New York Rangers,
Philadelphia, Pittsburgh, Washington.

NHL teams

Boston Bruins: Joined the NHL in 1924.
                        Have won the Stanley Cup 5 times.

Buffalo Sabres: Joined the NHL in 1970.
Have never won the Stanley Cup.

Calgary Flames: Joined the NHL in 1972 as the
Atlanta Flames. Moved to Calgary
in 1980.
Have won the Stanley Cup once.

Chicago Black Hawks: Joined the NHL in 1926.
Have won the Stanley Cup 3 times.

Detroit Red Wings: Joined the NHL in 1926.
Have won the Stanley Cup 7 times.

Edmonton Oilers: Joined the NHL in 1979 when the
WHA folded.
Have won the Stanley Cup 5 times.

Hartford Whalers: Joined the NHL in 1979 when the
WHA folded.
Have never won the Stanley Cup.

Los Angeles Kings: Joined the NHL in 1967.
Have never won the Stanley Cup.

Minnesota North Stars: Joined the NHL in 1967.
Have never won the Stanley Cup.

Montreal Canadiens: Original member of the NHL.
Have won the Stanley Cup 22 times.

New Jersey Devils: Joined the NHL in 1974 as the Kansas City Scouts. Have moved twice, first in 1976 from Kansas City to Denver, where they became the Colorado Rockies, and then in 1982 to New Jersey. Have never won the Stanley Cup.

New York Islanders: Joined the NHL in 1972
Have won the Stanley Cup 4 times.

New York Rangers: Joined the NHL in 1926.
Have won the Stanley Cup 3 times.

Philadelphia Flyers: Joined the NHL in 1967.
Have won the Stanley Cup twice.

Pittsburgh Penguins: Joined the NHL in 1967.
Have won the Stanley Cup once.

Quebec Nordiques: Joined the NHL in 1979 when the WHA folded.
Have never won the Stanley Cup.

St Louis Blues: Joined the NHL in 1967.
Have never won the Stanley Cup.

Toronto Maple Leafs: Original member of the NHL.
Have won the Stanley Cup 13 times.

Vancouver Canucks: Joined the NHL in 1970.
Have never won the Stanley Cup.

Washington Capitals: Joined the NHL in 1974.
Have never won the Stanley Cup.

Winnipeg Jets: Joined the NHL in 1979 when the WHA folded.
Have never won the Stanley Cup.

NHL Players' Association (NHLPA): The players' union.

Nationalities: Canadians continue to dominate professional hockey through Canada's countless school and junior leagues, as well as some semi-professional leagues.

American junior hockey is not as well organized, with the exception of a few regions in the northeast near the Canadian border.

In 1988, 76% of NHL players were Canadian, 14% American, and 10% European.

For the past five or six years, the number of Europeans has been constant, but as eastern Europe opens up, the numbers will increase. Czechs can now leave freely, and Soviet players can obtain special permission to leave the country when they reach 27 years old.

No-trade Clause: A clause in a player's contract that prohibits his trade without his approval.

One-way Contract, Two-way Contract: A one-way contract means that a player receives the same salary and bonuses whether he plays in the NHL or is transferred to a farm team.

A two-way contract means that a player takes a pay cut, sometimes as much as 40 to 50%, if he is sent down to the minor leagues.

Option year: In the year following the end of a player's contract, his club is entitled to his services if the club matches any offer by another team.

Playoffs: Post-season finals. Sixteen teams make the play-offs in the NHL. The winner of each division meets the fourth-place team, while the second-place team meets the third-place. Winners of each series play each other, first in division finals, then conference finals, and ultimately in a best-of-seven match-up for the Stanley Cup.

President: The chief executive officer of the NHL. Currently, John A. Ziegler is president. He is the fourth president, and the first American, since the formation of the NHL.

Rookie: A first-year player.

Scout: Someone who follows and observes young, promising players. All NHL clubs have their own scouts in North America and Europe. As well, the NHL runs the Central Scouting Bureau, which supplies general player information to all clubs.

Standing ovation: When the crowd stands and applauds a player, coach or team.

Stanley Cup: The winner of the NHL playoffs receives the Stanley Cup, a trophy donated to hockey in 1893 by Lord Stanley of Preston. Originally, the cup went to the best amateur team in Canada. Until 1926, the winners of all leagues, both amateur and professional, competed for the Stanley Cup, but since then, it has been awarded only to NHL teams. The Stanley Cup has been presented every year since 1893, except for 1919 when an influenza epidemic forced an end to the challenge match.

Stanley Cup winners over the years:

1918: Toronto Arenas
1919: —
1920: Ottawa Senators
1921: Ottawa Senators
1922: Toronto St. Patricks
1923: Ottawa Senators
1924: Montreal Canadiens
1925: Victoria Cougars
1926: Montreal Maroons
1927: Ottawa Senators
1928: New York Rangers
1929: Boston Bruins
1930: Montreal Canadiens
1931: Montreal Canadiens
1932: Toronto Maple Leafs
1933: New York Rangers
1934: Chicago Black Hawks
1935: Montreal Maroons
1936: Detroit Red Wings
1937: Detroit Red Wings
1938: Chicago Black Hawks
1939: Boston Bruins
1940: New York Rangers
1941: Boston Bruins
1942: Toronto Maple Leafs
1943: Detroit Red Wings
1944: Montreal Canadiens
1945: Toronto Maple Leafs
1946: Montreal Canadiens
1947: Toronto Maple Leafs
1948: Toronto Maple Leafs
1949: Toronto Maple Leafs
1950: Detroit Red Wings
1951: Toronto Maple Leafs
1952: Detroit Red Wings
1953: Montreal Canadiens
1954: Detroit Red Wings

1955: Detroit Red Wings
1956: Montreal Canadiens
1957: Montreal Canadiens
1958: Montreal Canadiens
1959: Montreal Canadiens
1960: Montreal Canadiens
1961: Chicago Black Hawks
1962: Toronto Maple Leafs
1963: Toronto Maple Leafs
1964: Toronto Maple Leafs
1965: Montreal Canadiens
1966: Montreal Canadiens
1967: Toronto Maple Leafs
1968: Montreal Canadiens
1969: Montreal Canadiens
1970: Boston Bruins
1971: Montreal Canadiens
1972: Boston Bruins
1973: Montreal Canadiens
1974: Philadelphia Flyers
1975: Philadelphia Flyers
1976: Montreal Canadiens
1977: Montreal Canadiens
1978: Montreal Canadiens
1979: Montreal Canadiens
1980: New York Islanders
1981: New York Islanders
1982: New York Islanders
1983: New York Islanders
1984: Edmonton Oilers
1985: Edmonton Oilers
1986: Montreal Canadiens
1987: Edmonton Oilers
1988: Edmonton Oilers
1989: Calgary Flames
1990: Edmonton Oilers
1991: Pittsburgh Penguins

Trade: To sell or transfer a player to another team.

World Hockey Association (WHA): A rival league to the NHL, founded in 1972 by two American businessmen. Originally made up of twelve teams, the WHA generated quick publicity by offering huge contracts to several NHL stars. The two most spectacular signings were of Bobby Hull, by the Winnipeg Jets, and Gordie Howe, who came out of retirement to play with his sons Marty and Mark for the Houston Aeros. Without the legitimacy provided by these stars, the new league would probably have folded before the beginning of the first season. Instead, the two leagues began a bidding war in which many NHL and WHA clubs were brought to their knees financially.

The league was never able to achieve stability. Teams joined, moved cities, and disappeared with unfortunate regularity. By the time it folded, only six teams remained and only four, the New England Whalers, Quebec Nordiques, Winnipeg Jets, and Edmonton Oilers, could afford the $6 million fee to join the NHL. When they did, in March, 1979, the NHL's most serious rival was dead.

Facts About the Canada Cup

Canada Cup '76 — September 2-15

Canada 11—Finland 2

Sweden 5—USA 2

Czechoslovakia 5—Soviet Union 3

Sweden 3—Soviet Union 3

Canada 4—USA 2

Czechoslovakia 8—Finland 0

Soviet Union 11—Finland 0

Czechoslovakia 4—USA 4

Canada 4—Sweden 0

Finland 8—Sweden 6

Soviet Union 5—USA 0

Czechoslovakia 1—Canada 0

USA 6—Finland 3

Sweden 2—Czechoslovakia 1

Canada 3—Soviet Union 1

Börje Salming

Final standings

	Gm	W	T	L	Gf Ga	Pts *
Canada	5	4	0	1	22-6	8
Czechoslovakia	5	3	1	1	19-9	7
Soviet Union	5	2	1	2	23-14	5
Sweden	5	2	1	2	16-18	5
USA	5	1	1	3	14-21	3
Finland	5	1	0	4	16-42	2

* Gm–Games, W–Wins, T–Ties, L–Losses, Gf–Goals for, Ga–Goals against, Pts–Points

Playoffs
Canada 6—Czechoslovakia 0
Canada 5—Czechoslovakia 4

Canada Cup '81 — September 1-13

Canada 9—Finland 0
USA 3—Sweden 1
Soviet Union 1—Czechoslovakia 1
Canada 8—USA 3
Czechoslovakia 7—Finland 1
Soviet Union 6—Sweden 3
Canada 4—Czechoslovakia 4
Sweden 5—Finland 0
Soviet Union 4—USA 1
Canada 4—Sweden 3
USA 6—Czechoslovakia 2
Soviet Union 6—Finland 1
Canada 7—Soviet Union 3
Finland 4—USA 4
Czechoslovakia 7—Sweden 1

Final Standings

	Gm	W	T	L	Gf Ga	Pts *
Canada	5	4	1	0	32-13	9
Soviet Union	5	3	1	1	20-13	7
Czechoslovakia	5	2	2	1	21-13	6
USA	5	2	1	2	17-19	5
Sweden	5	1	0	4	13-20	2
Finland	5	0	1	4	6-31	1

* Gm–Games, W–Wins, T–Ties, L–Losses, Gf–Goals for, Ga–Goals against, Pts–Points

Semi-finals
Soviet Union 4—Czechoslovakia 1
Canada 4—USA 1

Final
Soviet Union 8—Canada 1

Börje's Career in Figures

The NHL

Year	Team	Regular Season				Playoffs			
		Gm	G	A	Pm	Gm	G	A	Pm*
1973-74	Toronto	76	5	34	48	4	0	1	4
1974-75	Toronto	60	12	25	34	7	0	4	6
1975-76	Toronto	78	16	41	70	10	3	4	9
1976-77	Toronto	76	12	66	46	9	3	6	6
1977-78	Toronto	80	16	60	70	6	2	2	6
1978-79	Toronto	78	17	56	76	6	0	1	8
1979-80	Toronto	74	19	52	94	3	1	1	2
1980-81	Toronto	72	5	61	154	3	0	2	4
1981-82	Toronto	69	12	44	170	–	–	–	–
1982-83	Toronto	69	7	38	104	4	1	4	10
1983-84	Toronto	68	5	38	92	–	–	–	–
1984-85	Toronto	73	6	33	76	–	–	–	–
1985-86	Toronto	41	7	15	48	10	1	6	14

Year	Team	Regular Season				Playoffs			
		Gm	G	A	Pm	Gm	G	A	Pm*
1986-87	Toronto	56	4	16	42	13	0	3	14
1987-88	Toronto	66	2	24	82	6	1	3	8
1988-89	Toronto	63	3	17	86	–	–	–	–
1989-90	Detroit	49	2	17	52	–	–	–	–

Totals: 1,229 games, 162 goals, 674 assists, 1,435 penalty minutes.

* Gm - Games, G - Goals, A - Assists, Pm - Penalty minutes

The rest of his career

1967-68   Kiruna AIF div II (8 games)
           The TV-Puck, Norrbotten (2 games)**

1968-69   Kiruna AIF div II (13 games)
           Junior national team (11 games, 1 goal,
           Junior European Cup—silver)

1969-70   Kiruna AIF div II (16 games, 5 goals)
           Junior national team (13 games, 2 goals, Junior
           European Cup—bronze)

1970-71   Brynäs IF Swedish series (allsvenskan)
           (27 games, 2 goals, 6 assists, 22 penalty min-
           utes, Swedish champions)
           National B team (7 games, 1 goal)

** Swedish television broadcasts a national competition for district junior teams, called **TV-Puck-Team**.

1971-72   Brynäs IF Swedish series (Swedish champions)
          National B team (3 games)
          Tre Kronor* (12 games, World Cup—bronze)

1972-73   Brynäs IF Swedish series
          Tre Kronor (23 games, 4 goals, World Cup—silver)

1976-77   Tre Kronor (fourth place in Canada Cup)

1981-82   Tre Kronor (fifth place in Canada Cup)

1988-89   Tre Kronor (fourth place in World Cup)

1990-   Solna AIK

Individual Achievements

1970   Div II: Norrbotten's most valuable player

1971-72   Div I: Best player in 10 games

1972-73   Div I: Best player in 17 games, the highest
          number of all players. Ulf Sterner was second
          with 14 games.

1973-74   Member of the All-Star Team in the World Cup;
          NHL: winner of the Molson Cup as the most
          valuable Leaf

1974-75   NHL: second All-Star selection

---

* Three Crowns (National A-team)

1975-76   NHL: second All-Star selection

1976-77   NHL: first All-Star selection; winner of the
Molson Cup
Canada Cup: All-Star selection

1977-78   NHL: second All-Star selection; winner of the
Molson Cup

1978-79   NHL: second All-Star selection

1979-80   NHL: second All-Star selection; winner of the
Molson Cup

1982   NHL: awarded the Charlie Conacher Trophy
for great humanitarian contributions off the ice

1989   NHL: broke the Toronto record for most assists
in a career (620)

Index
of Names

H

Hammarström, Inge, 42, 49, 86, 101, 171
Harris, Billy, 42, 81
Hedberg, Anders, 23-24, 48, 113, 116, 163, 165
Helander, Peter, 119
Henderson, Paul, 37, 39, 80-81, 86
Henning, Lorne, 91, 93, 154
Homqvist, Leif "Honken", 24, 49
Hull, Bobby, 96, 116
Hutchison, Dave, 72, 86
Högosta, Göran, 115, 117

I

Imlach, Leonard "Punch", 94, 97, 124-130, 160-161

J

Jakusjev, Alexander, 36
Jansson, Henry, 26-27, 59-60

K

Karlsson, Stefan "Lill-Prosten", 35, 40, 169
Kelly, Red, 63, 76-78, 81, 85-89, 109
Kelly, Bob, 68
Keon, Dave, 65, 88, 101
Kinnear, Guy, 66, 156

L

Labraaten, Dan, 113
Lantto, Rune, 13-14, 26-27

Lemelin, Dan, 156
Lindberg, Hans "Virus", 113, 117
Lundström, Tord, 35, 49

M

MacLeish, Rick, 87
MacMillan, Yolanda, 140
Mahovlich, Frank, 37
Mahovlich, Pete, 37
Maloney, Dan, 17
Maltsev, Alexander, 36
McDonald, Lanny, 72, 86, 91-92, 94-95, 125-126
McKenny, Jim, 76, 86
McNamara, Gerry, 41-42, 45-46, 49-50, 55, 130
Michailov, Boris, 36, 50
Mikita, Stan, 37
Moroney, Des, 32, 42

N

Neal, John, 64-65, 76, 160
Neely, Bob, 62
Neilson, Roger, 18, 89-90, 121-124, 137
Nilsson, Henning, 21, 26
Nilsson, Kent, 129
Nilsson, Lars-Göran, 22, 35, 115
Nilsson, Ulf, 24, 35, 51, 113, 118
Nishimoto, Harry, 160
Norris, Bruce, 48
Nykoluk, Mike, 17, 130

O

Orr, Bobby, 37, 119

P

Palmateer, Mike, 86, 90-91, 127
Parent, Bernie, 70
Park, Brad, 37
Petrov, Vladimir, 36
Proudfoot, Jim, 66

R

Ragulin, Alexandr, 36
Reagan, Ronald, 104

S

Saleski, Don, 68
Salming, Anders N., 11
Salming, Anders, 82, 85, 88, 97, 149, 165
Salming, Carina, 12
Salming, Erland, 10
Salming, Isak, 12
Salming, Karin (Börje's mother), 10-13, 22, 26, 101
Salming, Lena, 29
Salming, Margitta, 40, 54-58, 75-76, 79-80, 82, 85, 104, 140, 149-150, 155, 158, 164, 167
Salming, Stig, 7, 9-12, 14, 18, 21-22, 24, 29-30, 32-33, 38-39, 41-42, 81-82, 148
Salming, Teresa, 82, 85, 97, 128, 149, 165
Sandlin, Tommy, 18, 30, 53-54
Schultz, Dave, 67-68, 79
Sittler, Darryl, 70, 72, 85-86, 101, 118, 122, 125-127, 129

Sjöberg, Lars-Erik, 35, 113, 117
Smith, Floyd, 125
Smith, Kate, 87
Smythe, Conn, 134-135
Stephenson, Wayne, 87
Sterner, Ulf, 34-35, 38, 44, 49, 51, 171
Sundström, Patrik, 119
Svensson, Kjell, 38, 44, 50, 53

T

Thompson, Errol, 86
Tretiak, Vladislav, 36, 116
Turnbull, Ian, 63, 66, 86, 91

V

Vachon, Rogatien, 116
Vasiljev, Valerij, 36

W

Wagnsson, Björn, 43, 45-47, 49, 52-53, 55, 59-60, 81-82, 105, 118-119, 129
Watson, Joe, 68
Wickberg, Thure, 22, 27, 29, 33, 59-60
Wickberg, Håkan, 29, 35
Williams, Tiger, 68, 70, 86, 139
Woods, Bob, 42
Ziegler, John, 146